[Divine meditations.] (1572)

Thomas Palfreyman

Early English Books Online (EEBO) Editions

Imagine holding history in your hands.

Now you can. Digitally preserved and previously accessible only through libraries as Early English Books Online, this rare material is now available in single print editions. Thousands of books written between 1475 and 1700 and ranging from religion to astronomy, medicine to music, can be delivered to your doorstep in individual volumes of high-quality historical reproductions.

We have been compiling these historic treasures for more than 70 years. Long before such a thing as "digital" even existed, ProQuest founder Eugene Power began the noble task of preserving the British Museum's collection on microfilm. He then sought out other rare and endangered titles, providing unparalleled access to these works and collaborating with the world's top academic institutions to make them widely available for the first time. This project furthers that original vision.

These texts have now made the full journey -- from their original printing-press versions available only in rare-book rooms to online library access to new single volumes made possible by the partnership between artifact preservation and modern printing technology. A portion of the proceeds from every book sold supports the libraries and institutions that made this collection possible, and that still work to preserve these invaluable treasures passed down through time.

This is history, traveling through time since the dawn of printing to your own personal library.

Initial Proquest EEBO Print Editions collections include:

Early Literature

This comprehensive collection begins with the famous Elizabethan Era that saw such literary giants as Chaucer, Shakespeare and Marlowe, as well as the introduction of the sonnet. Traveling through Jacobean and Restoration literature, the highlight of this series is the Pollard and Redgrave 1475-1640 selection of the rarest works from the English Renaissance.

Early Documents of World History

This collection combines early English perspectives on world history with documentation of Parliament records, royal decrees and military documents that reveal the delicate balance of Church and State in early English government. For social historians, almanacs and calendars offer insight into daily life of common citizens. This exhaustively complete series presents a thorough picture of history through the English Civil War.

Historical Almanacs

Historically, almanacs served a variety of purposes from the more practical, such as planting and harvesting crops and plotting nautical routes, to predicting the future through the movements of the stars. This collection provides a wide range of consecutive years of "almanacks" and calendars that depict a vast array of everyday life as it was several hundred years ago.

Early History of Astronomy & Space

Humankind has studied the skies for centuries, seeking to find our place in the universe. Some of the most important discoveries in the field of astronomy were made in these texts recorded by ancient stargazers, but almost as impactful were the perspectives of those who considered their discoveries to be heresy. Any independent astronomer will find this an invaluable collection of titles arguing the truth of the cosmic system.

Early History of Industry & Science

Acting as a kind of historical Wall Street, this collection of industry manuals and records explores the thriving industries of construction; textile, especially wool and linen; salt; livestock; and many more.

Early English Wit, Poetry & Satire

The power of literary device was never more in its prime than during this period of history, where a wide array of political and religious satire mocked the status quo and poetry called humankind to transcend the rigors of daily life through love, God or principle. This series comments on historical patterns of the human condition that are still visible today.

Early English Drama & Theatre

This collection needs no introduction, combining the works of some of the greatest canonical writers of all time, including many plays composed for royalty such as Queen Elizabeth I and King Edward VI. In addition, this series includes history and criticism of drama, as well as examinations of technique.

Early History of Travel & Geography

Offering a fascinating view into the perception of the world during the sixteenth and seventeenth centuries, this collection includes accounts of Columbus's discovery of the Americas and encompasses most of the Age of Discovery, during which Europeans and their descendants intensively explored and mapped the world. This series is a wealth of information from some the most groundbreaking explorers.

Early Fables & Fairy Tales

This series includes many translations, some illustrated, of some of the most well-known mythologies of today, including Aesop's Fables and English fairy tales, as well as many Greek, Latin and even Oriental parables and criticism and interpretation on the subject.

Early Documents of Language & Linguistics

The evolution of English and foreign languages is documented in these original texts studying and recording early philology from the study of a variety of languages including Greek, Latin and Chinese, as well as multilingual volumes, to current slang and obscure words. Translations from Latin, Hebrew and Aramaic, grammar treatises and even dictionaries and guides to translation make this collection rich in cultures from around the world.

Early History of the Law

With extensive collections of land tenure and business law "forms" in Great Britain, this is a comprehensive resource for all kinds of early English legal precedents from feudal to constitutional law, Jewish and Jesuit law, laws about public finance to food supply and forestry, and even "immoral conditions." An abundance of law dictionaries, philosophy and history and criticism completes this series.

Early History of Kings, Queens and Royalty

This collection includes debates on the divine right of kings, royal statutes and proclamations, and political ballads and songs as related to a number of English kings and queens, with notable concentrations on foreign rulers King Louis IX and King Louis XIV of France, and King Philip II of Spain. Writings on ancient rulers and royal tradition focus on Scottish and Roman kings, Cleopatra and the Biblical kings Nebuchadnezzar and Solomon.

Early History of Love, Marriage & Sex

Human relationships intrigued and baffled thinkers and writers well before the postmodern age of psychology and self-help. Now readers can access the insights and intricacies of Anglo-Saxon interactions in sex and love, marriage and politics, and the truth that lies somewhere in between action and thought.

Early History of Medicine, Health & Disease

This series includes fascinating studies on the human brain from as early as the 16th century, as well as early studies on the physiological effects of tobacco use. Anatomy texts, medical treatises and wound treatment are also discussed, revealing the exponential development of medical theory and practice over more than two hundred years.

Early History of Logic, Science and Math

The "hard sciences" developed exponentially during the 16th and 17th centuries, both relying upon centuries of tradition and adding to the foundation of modern application, as is evidenced by this extensive collection. This is a rich collection of practical mathematics as applied to business, carpentry and geography as well as explorations of mathematical instruments and arithmetic; logic and logicians such as Aristotle and Socrates; and a number of scientific disciplines from natural history to physics.

Early History of Military, War and Weaponry

Any professional or amateur student of war will thrill at the untold riches in this collection of war theory and practice in the early Western World. The Age of Discovery and Enlightenment was also a time of great political and religious unrest, revealed in accounts of conflicts such as the Wars of the Roses.

Early History of Food

This collection combines the commercial aspects of food handling, preservation and supply to the more specific aspects of canning and preserving, meat carving, brewing beer and even candy-making with fruits and flowers, with a large resource of cookery and recipe books. Not to be forgotten is a "the great eater of Kent," a study in food habits.

Early History of Religion

From the beginning of recorded history we have looked to the heavens for inspiration and guidance. In these early religious documents, sermons, and pamphlets, we see the spiritual impact on the lives of both royalty and the commoner. We also get insights into a clergy that was growing ever more powerful as a political force. This is one of the world's largest collections of religious works of this type, revealing much about our interpretation of the modern church and spirituality.

Early Social Customs

Social customs, human interaction and leisure are the driving force of any culture. These unique and quirky works give us a glimpse of interesting aspects of day-to-day life as it existed in an earlier time. With books on games, sports, traditions, festivals, and hobbies it is one of the most fascinating collections in the series.

The BiblioLife Network

This project was made possible in part by the BiblioLife Network (BLN), a project aimed at addressing some of the huge challenges facing book preservationists around the world. The BLN includes libraries, library networks, archives, subject matter experts, online communities and library service providers. We believe every book ever published should be available as a high-quality print reproduction; printed on-demand anywhere in the world. This insures the ongoing accessibility of the content and helps generate sustainable revenue for the libraries and organizations that work to preserve these important materials.

The following book is in the "public domain" and represents an authentic reproduction of the text as printed by the original publisher. While we have attempted to accurately maintain the integrity of the original work, there are sometimes problems with the original work or the micro-film from which the books were digitized. This can result in minor errors in reproduction. Possible imperfections include missing and blurred pages, poor pictures, markings and other reproduction issues beyond our control. Because this work is culturally important, we have made it available as part of our commitment to protecting, preserving, and promoting the world's literature.

GUIDE TO FOLD-OUTS MAPS and OVERSIZED IMAGES

The book you are reading was digitized from microfilm captured over the past thirty to forty years. Years after the creation of the original microfilm, the book was converted to digital files and made available in an online database.

In an online database, page images do not need to conform to the size restrictions found in a printed book. When converting these images back into a printed bound book, the page sizes are standardized in ways that maintain the detail of the original. For large images, such as fold-out maps, the original page image is split into two or more pages

Guidelines used to determine how to split the page image follows:

- Some images are split vertically; large images require vertical and horizontal splits.
- For horizontal splits, the content is split left to right.
- For vertical splits, the content is split from top to bottom.
- For both vertical and horizontal splits, the image is processed from top left to bottom right.

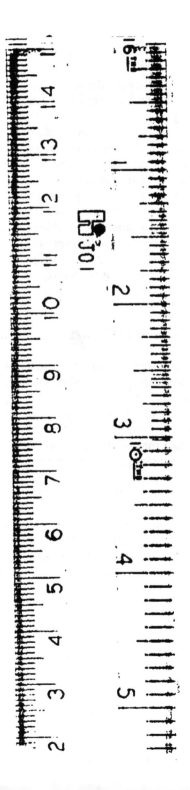

¶To the righte wor-
shipful, Maistresse Isabel Harington,
one of the Gentlewomen of the Queenes
Maiesties most honorable priuie Chamber,
Thomas Paulfreyman hir dayly Orator
wisheth (with continuance) the in-
crease of Gods eternal grace
and fauour.

AS EXPERIENCE
playnely teacheth,
tyme truely telleth,
and nature for the
moste parte appro-
ueth the diuersitie
of our humane affects in diet : hovv
not only to the vvorshipful or most
honorable, but also to the very poo-
rest and of most base estate, the deli-
catest, most deintie, svvete and pleasant dishes, are not alvvayes aptely
agreable, or to contente fully their
minds, but sometimes for a shift and
to their better liking, desireth more
ordinarie, grosse and familiar fare :
vvherby in nature they are the bet-

*.ij.   ter

ter contented, their appetites ofte
times more quickened, their minds
recreated, yea, and the healthes of
their bodies the better also preser-
ued: euen so (righte vvorshipfull)
touching the interne parte, diuine
substance or invvarde affections of
the soule: the heauenly nature also
and most christen diet therof, experience and tyme beareth likevvyse
their svvay, effectually to iudge and
declare the same in truth, among the
sounde members of Chrystes onely
immaculate, most preciouse and vn
spotted body, to their sufficient con-
tentation, quickning, recreating, and
most healthfull preseruing. And al-
beit you are herein for your part, as
the electe of God surely grounded
in him of good purpose foreap-
poynted, and by grace moste happely called, to be in this life (vvyth
prepared soule and quiet cōscience)
partaker

partaker of sundry his heauenly de
licates, accustomably norished, most
dayntely sedde, and abundauntly satisfied, to your very vvell lyking, in
the excellencie of such your ioyouse
and invvarde refection: and vvithout
ouer secret hiding, a knovven distri-
butor of your good portion to o-
thers, for their bothe bodily and
ghostly comforte at all times in necessitie, as the shevver fauourably
foorth the flovving frutes of fayth-
fulnesse and true pietie : yet presu-
ming vpon your vertue and christen
clemencie, I haue novve boldly attempted and moste humbly cōmen-
ded vnto you (for varieties sake)
this moste vnvvorthy, very slender,
and ouer base present, to be at the
least by your godly sufferaunce (as
superfluous store amōg the rest) but
a backestander in your sight, to bee
looked vpon aloofe, a long and sarre

*.iij. off,

off, as it vvere but by the vvay, euen
vvith a glauncing eye, and at leisure
to be tryed for your onely pleasure,
vvhat is the effectuall and true taast
therof. but not to alienate or alter by
any meanes, your already vvel staied
and moft happy affections, so mightily confirmed in you (and that in
the beft parte) by the ineffable povver of Gods mofte sacred spirite,
your only and omnisufficient piller:
but rather in dede to incitate you (if
poffibly it might be) to the better
eftimatiō of your ovvn former pro-
uifion, and moft faultlefle fornamed
furniture. And truely greate reafon
vvhy it should be so, that things vvel
knovven, and of mofte excellencie,
should haue condignely their befte
preferment : for fo God him felfe
vvith the moft godly, vvould vvishe
by iuftice it should fo be, hovv foe-
uer moft cōmonly they are knovvne
to

to the contrarie. And notvvithstan-
ding the dayes are novve diuersly
daungerous, very dayntie, and exceede in muche tyneneſſe, vvhether
in ſpeaking, curiouſe deuiſing, ex-
acte ſearching or penning of matter, touching either diuinitie or o-
thervvyſe of Prophane deſcripti-
ons : ſo very ſinguler, exquiſite,
pycked, and tender are mens eares,
naturally adioyned to their flouri-
ſhing, quicke, and ready vvyttes,
profounde knovvledge and iudgemente ! and therefore the more ha-
ſardefull, and a meane truely to purchaſe vnto themſelues that deale in
ſuche caſes, rather reprochefull and
many ſcorneſull ſcoffes, than com-
mendation or ſhevv of good countenance, vnleſſe they rarely exceede
or ſurmount the vvel dooings of infinite others: and that alſo (touching
thys my preſente attempt (vvheras

*.iiij.   the

the godly in thefe dayes, hath mofte
gratioufly endeuored to fet forth already, and that mofte plentifully, diuers and fondry vvorks, very diuine-
ly, of great excellency, and of necef-
fitie, to quicken and ftirre vp daily to
God, the ouer droufie, flacke, & fick
finnefull foules, to reioyce alfo their
mindes, and to fructifie before him,
their vnprofitable and baraine harts:
yet as a pore helper, a moft inferiour
labourer, or vvell vvilling drudge in
the vineyarde of Chrifte, humbling
my felfe moft gladly, vnder the correction of the charitable and frendly, of the godly vvife in their knovvn
vertue and humbleneffe, approued
skilfulneffe, vvatchfulneffe, and nee-
die diligence, in that their holy fun-
ction appointed : beholding vvith
them the neceffity of the time, hovv
the vvilde vveedes of vvilfulneffe to
vvickedneffe, finne and abhomination,

on, do daily abound and raign rank-
ly vvithout sufficient stoppe, in their
very infectuous and filthie fulnesse,
to choke, to represse and kepe lovve
by the grounde, the fragraunte and
svveete smelling fruites of vertue :
vvhereby, as vvith infinite snares, the
Diuell entangleth, still daily encrea-
seth, infecteth, poisoneth, and hazar-
deth all the leudly idle, carelesse and
vaine children of this so sore crazed
and old stouping vvorld of deth (al-
redie iudged, condemned, and at the
brink of deth:) in vvhom, by vvhom,
and during vvhose time, Satan tempteth, allureth, deceiueth, pluketh to-
vvardes him, and tosseth them as it
seemeth vvith his cruell clavves, vp
side dovvne at his pleasure, and dali-
eth vvith them at his vvill, as vvith
his ovvne possessed, as vvith those
that forsake God, as in a time of the
contempt of god, of hating the clere

x. v.   light

light of god, of louing the darknesse
of the diuel to their condempnation
more than the light, of selfe loue, of
pride and vanitie, of defiled life, and
suche like : a time approued of all
times, most straunge, most monstru-
ous, and therefore the more daungerous: wherby sathan with his whole
rablement of hellike ministers, the
world also it selfe, and the proud rebellious flesh, mainly bestirreth the
with their full povver togither, to
make hauock, & to bring altogither
vnder their seruile, most confused &
bitter yoke: I haue in my moste simple vnderstanding, and as God therin
by his grace hath directed me, endeuored to bestovve some parte of my
time, in setting forthe sundry godly
meditations and prayers, vpon speci-
al causes respected, as instrumentes,
to shrub, to roote out, cutte dovvne,
spoile and destroy, at the least some
poy

poyſoned euils, from the moſt beautiful and louely vineyard of Chriſte.
And as I haue by them thought moſt
conuenient, that oure almightie and
moſt terrible God (vvho ſeemeth to
be greatly amongſt vs forgotten) in
euery of them ſhuld cheeſely be had
in remembrance, to be duely reuerē-
ced and feared, to be called vpon and
moſt highly magnified: ſo haue I for
the moſt part, made mention of our
frailetie, preſent and moſt vvretched
ſtate, and of the mightie povver alſo
of our forſaid enemies, hovv politike
they are, hovv puiſſant, hovv vvatch-
ful, hovv cruel, hovv accuſtomably in
all eſtates they do preuaile, and that
God therfore by humble ſute vvold
ſone graunt vs his mercy, extēd forth
his arme to ſtrengthen vs, and moſte
gratiouſly in time deliuer vs: leaſt in
the vvaightineſſe of our ſins yet daily
amongſte vs encreaſed, vve be ouer
ſore

fore preſſed, oure conſciences moſte
fovvly defiled, burdened, depely gal-
led and vvounded, the iudgementes
of the higheſt not vvayed, oure in-
vvard ſenſes benummed, oure hartes
hardened, all diuine graces contemned, and ſo vvith the plages of God,
the more ſvviftly by his iuſtice confounded: heaping in the vvhile vége-
ance vpõ our ſelues, againſt the day
of his vvrathe and publike declarati-
on, of his proclaimed and iuſt iudgement, and to be dampned vvith the
vvorld, vvith the Diuell, and his Angels for euer: vnto vvhom, by vvhoſe
cuſtome, and importune knocking
at the doores of our graceleſſe, very
vaine, and moſt fruteleſſe hearts (the
knocking of the Lorde Chriſt vvil-
fully neglected) vvee haue ſubiected
oure ſelues, and opened vvide vnto
him, to let in both him ſelf, his con-
ioyned companions, and vvith them
all

all abhomination and vnrightuouse-
nesse, to quicken vvith more lust the
flames of Gods furie, to make pon-
derous and ouer heauie, the svvirfe
descending ballance, of his very terrible & irreuokeable iustice. To the
ende therefore, this small and moste
simple volume, may (vnder youre
godly protection) gather the rather
some estimation and credite, & passe
forth for good to the vse of the godly, I moste humbly beseeche youre
vvorship, so to accepte it in the simplicitie thereof, and graunt thereun-
to your Christian furtherance , that
some good for Goddes glory, may
grovve thereby to some, that some
liues at the least may be somevvhat
amended, the furies of God the soo
ner preuented, and the bright light e
of the sonne of god shine with more
povver amongste vs, to ouerthrovve
vs in his feare, to beate flatte to the
earth,

earth, our earthie and proude fleshe, and to vvaste soone or consume, for good and most happie chaunge, our most damnable vvorks of darknesse. I shall (as of bounden duetie, for this and for other the like causes deserued) most humbly pray for you, that God in mercie may euer blesse, both you, your moste vvorthy belo-ued in Christe, your of-spring, and vvhole familie.

Your humble and daily Oratoure,
THOMAS Paulfreyman.

An exhortation to
the christen Reader.

Eing mindful(de-
uout christian) of
god thine heauēly
father: and as best
beseemeth thee, an
earthly creature,
always to remēm-
ber thy maker, & that by a quickning
spirite in the inwarde and newe man,
commended vnto thee from aboue, tho-
rough the free grace of election in Iesus
Christ: by whom thou art new borne :
to whom thou art coupled a quick and
a lyuely member : with whom thou art
partaker of the Heauenly and diuine
nature: (euen the nature of God thine
eternall father:) In whom thine harte
is prepared towardes him: by whome
thou seekest most truly to knowe him :
most

An exhortation

Wherunto the eternal spirite stirreth the hearts of gods electe.

most earnestly to loue him : diligently to seeke him : faythfully to serue hym : most lowly to honour him : reuerently to feare and obey him : and so foorth as his only worde of truth most straightly prescribeth and precisely requireth of thee, of all people, and in all estates, thoroughout all generations. In his hygh magnificence, almightynesse, eternitie, great power and maiestie : to loue him in his benignitie, in his myldenesse, tendernesse, faithfulnesse, truth and greate mercie : to feare him in his lordly dignitie, princely gouernment, statelinesse, rough countenance, wrathefulnesse, seuere iustice and iudgement : and to offer daily vnto him, the acceptable sacrifice of faithfull and hartie prayers, in the name of his sonne Iesus Christe, as hee himselfe most healthfully taughte thee : and for whose onely sake, promyse is made to heare thee, that his myghtye hande may euer preserue thee, vphold thee,

thee, keepe thee safe, norishe thee, directe, strengthen, defende and deliuer thee, in all places, at all tymes, and in al cases of necessitie, bothe of bodye and soule : and to giue thee also thorough Christ, his holy spirite, as a seale of assurance, to certifie thee that thou arte the chyld of God, inwardly to inflame and comforte thee, to worke true faith into thee, to dispose with cheerfulnesse the frutes of true charitie, to quiet thee in al tempests of aduersitie: yea and to leade thee still on by the hande (for the tyme, and from time to tyme) vnto the place of rest, the cheerefull and safe porte, the restfull hauen or moste sure rode of eternal ioy and felicitie. If thou desire to enioy all these and suche lyke blessings as are moste needefull for thee (both for body and soul) from the hand of God, and according to the measure of the gift of Christ : O hearken then vnto the veyce of the Lord thy God:

⁎⁎   Incline

Incline humbly thine eare: prepare thine
hart: seeke him early in holinesse: turne
thee vnto him without delay: receyue
him with most pure affection: and lift
vp sone thy sickely soule, to beholde the
glory of his countenaunce. O bend thy
body of earth, downe to the face of the
earthe. Grone in thy selfe to God with
greefe, and lay open simply before him,
the felt secretes of thy sinful hart. Call
daily vppon him, and so aduisedly tru
him, as thou hast assured trust in him.
And before thou duetifully attemptest
thy godly contemplatiõs, prayers, praises, and thanks giuing to God: prepare
thee earnestly a fitte soule, for the pre
sence of so high and great a God. Forget not before whome thou presentest
thy selfe, and vnto whome thou doste
minde to talke. Be not vainly or wickedly presumptuous, in thine high and
great attempt before him. Abase thy
selfe: tremble in his presence. Remember

A preparation to Prayer.

Certaine spe-
cial causes fo-
lowing, that
are to be cõ-
sidred by gods
childrẽ, wher-
of they exa-
min thẽ selues
before prayer,
and receyuing
of the holy ta-

ber, god beholdeth al diforders in thee, cram nres, to
with a piercing, fharpe, and reuenging auoid his hea
eye. uy iudgemëts.

1 Examine therfore thy felfe before
with iudgemente. Defcende deeply
into thine owne bowells, and fee there,
whether thou be (as of ryghte thou
oughteft) truely penitent for thy former finnes and wickedneffe.

2 Whether thou determineft (thence
forth)from thine hearte, not to tourne
againe vnto them, as dothe a cleane
wafhed fwine, which newly defiles hir
felfe, in the lothfome and foule ftin-
king mire.

3 Whether thou bee in his fighte a
double faced or deepe diffembling hipo-
crite, touching thy dealings with him
and the worlde, as thy broke in thee of
records mofte playnely witneffith vnto thee.

4 Whether thou bee (as by name
thou profeffeft) a zelouse fauorer of

✱✱.iſ.   the

the word of life.

5 Whether thou (with the Prophet
Dauid) vnfeinedly hatest all super-
sticiouse vanities, contrary to the word
of life.

6 Whether thou (with the said pro-
phete) feelest in thy selfe to be grieued
with the enemies of God, and with all
such as rise vp ageinst him, or to suppresse the word of life.

7 Whether thou weyest wyth thy
selfe, that like as thy body, being but of
an earthy and corporall substaunce,
cannot possiblie liue without the vsual
nourishmente of materiall bread and
meate: so the soule, in the spirituall state
therof, cannot liue but be sterued and
dye (euen the eternall and euerlasting
deathe) withoute the spirituall nutri-
ment and heauenly sweete tast of the
woorde of God, whiche to the soule is
the onely breade of lyfe, and where-
after thou shouldest hunger, too vpholde

holde thy lyfe.

8 Whether thou stedfastly beleue to be saued, by the only merites, death and bloudshed of Christ crucified vpon the crosse, wwithoute thyne owne and other mens merites, eyther their most damnable and idolatrous dewised vanities.

9 Whether thou thynke'st it not the Dyuels bewytchyng, by his maligne ministers, to bee depriued of so pious and precious a prepared rauntsome.

10 Whether thou at the receyuing of the holy mysteries of Christes body and bloud, vnderstandest them to bee his owne only ordinance, for the vse of his holy churche, and to bee witnesses therein of the open and publike confession of the true faithe whiche thou haste in him, and to be saued onely by his bodilye death and the bloudy sacrifice vppon the Crosse, once for all

**.iij.   offerca

offered vnto God his heauenly father,
for thine, for mine, & for al the sinnes
of the whole worlde, euen so many, as
haue this acceptable faithe of God in
them.

11 Whether thou haue regarded by
the word of God (touching the Sacra-
ment of Christes body and blond) the
difference therin, betwixt the Diuelles
faith and thine, either the faithe of an
Hipocritishe and dampnable reprobate.

The diffrence
to be conside-
red betweene
the true chri-
stians fayth,
the faith of
the diuell, and
the reprobate

12 Whether thou hast by true faithe
repugned the Deuill, who boldely
chalengeth thee (as he thinketh he may
be bolde) and maketh equall comparison with thee of thy faithe, touching
simple the confession of Christe, as of
his Conception by the holy Ghost: of
his Natiuitie and birth of the virgine
Marie: to be also the Sonne of God.
liued perfecte and vndefiled man vppon the earthe, his doings to be onely
omni-

to the Reader.

omnipotent, most miraculous & wonderfull: suffered most sharpe and cruell
death: was buryed: rose againe, ascended into the heauens, verie God and
very man: yea, and of his retourne also
againe vnto iudgement. All these
things, the Diuels beleeue and confesse
with thee: but yet vtterly vnperswa-
ded, to be his onely sufficient sauioure
and redeemer, by his precious blowde
shedde and deathe: euen as those faithlesse wickednesse, which in theyr vn-
soundnesse, stubbornesse, & vnstayed
nesse, touching the couenant of God in
his sonne Christe, for their saluation,
accompt the price of his precious blond
to be insufficient for them, withoute the
very absurde and most fond annexing
of their owne and other mennes merites: and so to make Christe vnto
themselues, to be at the moste, but a
mingled, peeced, botched, and patchea
Sauioure.

** **.iiij.

An exhortation

13 Whether thou hast on this maner folowing considered of Sathans chalenge and comparison with thee, and sayde thus vnto hym in the secrecies of thy faithfull soule, for thy defence : O thou very mortal, most cruel and damned enemie, I vnfaynedly from myne hart defie thee : I withstande thee to the face: thou hast naught to doo with me, or to make suche comparisons with mee in my christen and most holy profession. I know full wel thy malice and stoutnesse, which hath ben in thee from the beginning, bothe agaynste the annoynted of God and all his. Experiēce teacheth me, of thy not slumbring, of thy wandring about, and seeking watchefully to deuoure and to spoyle mee of my faith, wherby I must be saued. I tell thee thou most wicked one, thy trauell is all in vayn. I am none of thyne, nor nothing inclined to thyne affection or motions. I am Gods I tell thee, and

The true chriſtiā at earneſt defiance with the diuel : and sheweth vnto him for his diſcoꝛagemēt the power of his fayth.

and the perſwaded childe of God by
his ſpirit of truth, who by grace poſ-
ſeſſing me, and by his power mightily
working in mee, hath moſte graciouſly
planted in my harte, the frutefull tree
of pietie, of true and perfect fayth, faſt
roted in me, deply ſtayed, and ſurely ſet
led, euen with the finger of god my father, touching the dignitie, price and
true eſtimation of his ſonne, and mine
onely ſauiours moſt preciouſe body, for
mine only health and eternal ſaluatiõ.
And though I haue falne or fainted,
as traiterouſly thou haſt tripped me,
yet of frailtie haue J falne, & not wilfully of malice, as thou haſte moſt ma-
liciouſly tempted me: which God hath
ſeene in me, in mercy therfore hath rai-
ſed me vp ageyne, and wil ſtil vpholde
me in ſpite of thee. Art thou ignorant
of this (thou griſeled and foule helly
monſter) that I am not ſuch a one as
thou art, or as thou woldeſt haue mee,

to bee doubtefull of my faythe, as the
wicked are, to leaue the freedome of
Gods spirite, and to bee entangled a-
gayne in thine infernall filthy bands?
Thinkeſt thou, that I beeyng nowe
called to the lighte and knowledge
of the ſweete woorde of life, whereof
I haue truely taſted, and haue in de-
teſtation mine olde conuerſation, will
be newly agayne deceiued, offer to approche, eyther once nibble or ſmell to
thy beſlubbered, brackiſhe, and moſt
filthy embrued baytes? Noteſt thou
me of ſuche ſlipperineſſe, that ha-
uyng farre entraunce in the ſpirite,
and feele the incomparable ioyes ther
of, that I will nowe ende in the greefes
and ſorrowes of the fleſhe? to ſitte
ſo lyttle by the Kyngdome of Ieſus
Chryſte, that taking holde of the
Plough, will now looke backe agayne,
to bee as a Dogge, and to returne
agayne to my vomite, or as a beaſte-
ly

ly Swyne, to beraye my selfe agayne
in the myre, to defourme the Image
of God, and to defile his holy Temple?
No no Sathan thou arte deceiued,
I tell thee truely for thy discourage-
mente, I am now better schooled, well
armed, and better warned, to let thee
goe for naughte. Knowest thou not
that I haue put vppon me to endure
for euer, my Lorde and God, my
Chryste and Sauioure? Art thou
forgetfull (O thou enemie) that I in
true faythe professing his name, and
receyuing woorthily hys holye and
most blessed Sacraments, by the onely
rule of his word, am armed ouer all,
with his only healthsul, and most mercifull merites, to strengthen me mightily ageinst thee: who is made mine with
all that he hathe: and I am onely hys,
both body and soule: one bodye wyth
him: fleshe of his fleshe, and bone of his
bones. Ah Sathan, this certeinty and
truethe

truth in faith considered, wastefull are
thy wretched wandringes and wylye
waightings to wreck and vex my soul.
Away from me, away I say thou cursed
and spightfull spirite : or stay if thou
lust to offer boldly vnto mee (as thou
darest) thy very blashlesse and bragge
attempts of malignitie. I yet tell thee,
they shall not hurt me: neither do I a-
ny thing esteeme thee: I regard not thy
force: I feare not thy fury: The Lorde
is my God: he is the God of my strēgth
and confidence : thou hast of thy selfe,
no powre at all ageinst me : For what
so euer thou attemptestc or seekest
to performe , therin to thy wil thou
wantest powre . But that which thou
doest, is by his onely omnipotent hande
and sufferaunce that is my God: whose
waight and mightinesse, thy broosed
braines hath silte, to make thee stoupe
for euer, to hamper thee at his will in
thine owne irons , to ouerthrowe thee

soun

soone in thine owne tourne, and to blowe
thee backewarde at will, euen with the
breath of his mouth, into the bailesse
and deepe botomelesse pitte : whose
bonde slaue thou art and a drudge enforced: and in thine outrage by his per-
miffion, a knowne peerelesse paricide, a
very restlesse, pitilesse, and most gracelesse raunging roge, the only ring lea-
der and infectuouse ranke roote of all
reproch, of all mischieues and abbomi-
nation vnder the sonne.

14 O beloued Christian: Whether
art thou in this wise armed with faith
too stande too the face of the Diuell,
sharply to reproue him, and put him to
flighte?

15 Whether hast thou in thine harte
through this faith, heauenly mirth and
melody, inward reioicing, and thy retourne with triumphe, exalted the
name of thy God, felt in thy selfe to bee
doubtlesse his childe, and too loue (as
thou

thou lawfully oughtest)the lawe of thy
deare and most louing father?

16 Whether hast thou considered
or not, this heauenly mistery aforesaid
to be the Sacramente of true pietie, the
Charaſter of perfeſte vnitie, and the
most aſſured band of frutful and chriſtian charitie?

17. Whether thou, being a subieſte
in any eſtate (borne to be ruled vnder
thy soueragne and not to rule) bearest
vnto hir thy dere and natural Prince
as also to thine natiue countrey (by the
bloud of Goddes woorde) a naturall,
faithfull, and true louing harte.

18 And finally, whether thou bee
chriſtianly charitable, or a cleere re-
mitter of all thy neighbours offences as
thou thy selfe woldeſt of God be clerely remitted. And ſo foorth in all other
thinges, as best behoueth thine holye
profeſſion: least to the cōtrary (in gods
ſighte) all thy conceyued holineſſe by
prayer

vraier or whatſoeuer, beeing but pro-
vhane, hipocritiſh, childiſh, mere dark
neſſe and very folly, there be founde in
thee, but the only title, or vnauailable
bare name of chriſtianitie: and therefore verie perniciouſe, hurtfull, and to
be tourned into ſinne ageinſt thee: and
ſo in ſtead of healthfull, very delight-
full, and beautifull bleſſings (which thou
daily huntest after) the banefull, moſt
bitter, and blacke curſes of God, doo
ſodeinly fall vppon thee. Beware then
I exhorte thee, looke well to thy ſelfe:
in time: flatter not thy ſelfe vainly or
rather dampnable: bē not longe a da-
lier, in the ſchoole houſe of daliaunce:
be not alwayes a fondling, a weakling,
or a ſuckling, a milkeſoppe, or babiſh
inſante in Chryſt: weye truely the
vertus of healthefull, manfull, and
ſtrong nouriſhmente in Chryſte, at-
tende to the tyme: thou ſhouldeſte
nowe bee a ſtrong man in Chryſte:
                                        thou

thou art now as a man most gratiously
visited, for the highest doo seeke thy
company: than the which, what shouldest thou more desire. O remember
then, how very reprochfull, how vnmā-
full, vnhealthfull, hurtfull, miserable,
and discōmendable, is thy seruile state,
in such wise to be pend in, not to growe
out in time, nor get from thy rockinges,
thy wearisome wrappinges, or swad
ling bandes of extreame weakenesse:
but alwayes to be lulde in the armes of
vntimely tendernesse, wherby thou art
barred from thy highest and moste
chiefe felicitie. Way warely by the scriptures, thy due danger and discommē-
dation, of suche thine insensibilitie and
wearishnesse. Shouldest not thou rather
reioice, to be calde as a man of strength
to the felowship, ripe age, and strong
manhode of Christe, and to be partaker in his presence, of his most frende-
full, healthfull, strengthfull, and heauē-
lye

to the Reader.

ly bankei?whereunto, al things are already prepared, and therunto art thou
now called. God also graunt thee, to be
in the number of his electe, that thou
maist with faith set forwards thy fore,
hungerly with zeale to striue for thy
place, & to beleue by Gods only word,
that the lord of the feast fauoreth thee.
Be not hindred, hinder not thy selfe,
let excuses be farre from thee, deferre
not the fauouring of thy soules refre-
shing, loke to thy turne in time, open to
day thine eyes, and be not yet blinde to
morowe, least with the blinde, in thy
wil of blindenesse, thou be sone blindely
led, into the irrecouerable, deepe, and
most damnable dungeon of blindnesse,
darknesse & horror, with the diuel, the
Prince of darknesse and death foreuer.
Consider this, he that seeth thee (euen
as in deede thou art) is a God of moste
cleare sighte, bright lighte, truthe and
rightuousnesse. Call to minde towardes

***   him

him, thy true profession & seruice: turn
not th   but of true kinde: leane simply t   truthe : ioyne not with the
wic   which by their questions dout
of that truth, and aske how knowe you
that it is the word of truth : for bothe
they & thou shall answer to that word
of truthe : whereby must be directed,
bothe thy religion and manners : and
wherin, thou must be bothe mindefull,
skilful and thākiful for thy discharge.
Ignoraunce cannot excuse thee, it shall
not excuse thee : thou oughtest not be
ignorant, thou nedest not be ignorant:
what so euer is writtē, is writtē for thy
learning: thou readest it, thou hearest
it, or thou maist if thou luste: It is not
farre from thee : It is before thine eyes
& in thine hart, if grace be with thee
towardes it, and is most truely pronoū-
ced vnto thee, by the eternall spirite of
truth, & that most miraculously with
al simplicitie, by his zealous ministers,
inwardly to pierce thee, to lighten the

darkneſſe of thine hart, and to quicken true life vnto thee, if thou haſte eares to heare in theſe dayes, the dayes of gods grace, and of his heauenly viſitation. Vaine curioſitie of faultes finding and complaining, ſhal not ſerue thee, in thy reſpecting of perſones, dayes and times: they oughte not to hinder thee: haue thou thine hart prepared, & ſtick thou to the graces of god offered. What are ſlanderous brutes to thee, if thou be of god & a louer of the truth: of which truthe, let thine owne conſcience be the iudge, if it be not vtterly dead, or moſt damnably benūmed. Whē thou heareſt the truth, in time take hold of truthe, let not occaſion ſlip from thee, with hir turnd baldneſſe towardes thee: for ſhee flieth ſwiftly, and to cal hir again back wil not help thee: yea, the truth wil thē reproue thie, be iuſte iudge ouer thee, and condempne thee to thy face, for thy moſte foliſhe and late repentaunce

If truthe therefore offer hir selfe vnto
thee, stand most amiably before thee,
and sound most heauenly words vnto
thine eare: O attend then to the truth,
haue good opinion in the truth, flie not
from the truthe, feare not the truthe
ioyne to the truth, be familiar with the
truth, beleue the truthe, confesse boldly
the truthe, and stand stedfastly to the
truth: for truthe is of high excellencie
a glorious ladie, a dame of noble fame,
and of great antiquitie: she is euer gratious vnto the frendly, of full power al
so, of great maiestie, and familiar with
the highest. Thinke well therefore of
truth, entertaine hir reuerently, shee
shineth with glory vnto thee. O let hir
alwayes possesse thee, reioyce in hir cō
panie, and vse hir very frendly, for she
wil highly againe requite thee, & shew
thee sone most freely, hir natural vsage
& propertie: which shalbe, all inward
ly to serch thee, thorowly to purge thee.
most

most clerely to polish thee, most beuti-
fully to adorne thee, to breake thy bāds
of impietie, to make the spiritually free
and prefer thee, through true faithe to
possesse the high presence of the deitie.
This is truthes nature, to deale kindly
with thee, if thou most vnkindly, neg-
lectest not hir companie. Of whiche
truth, the Apostle thus wryteth vnto
thee, that without al contradiction she
must nedes be vnto thee, either the sauoure of life vnto life: or the sauoure of
death vnto death. Such iudgemēt will
truth haue ouer thee, and stand in full
effect, there will be no meane, but to be
either with thee, or else flatly againste
thee, as it shall truely finde thee, at thy
fal frō this life. there wil be no daliāce:
it will for euer saue thee, or eternally
damne thee, how so euer thereof thou
makest thine account, or leanst of will
to the contrary, with thy very blinde,
wicked, and peruerse hart. Feare ther-

$* * *$.iij.   fore

fore, harken to the truth in time, haue
sure confidence in truthe, thine helper
is at hand, he and the truth are one, he
is grateful, he is faithful, dout thou not
double not, nor wilfully withstand not,
the offred graces of thy mylde master,
thy iust Lord, and moste louing God:
and be not before him, and in the presence of his holy Angels, vnprepared,
or a dallier, a man indifferent, a slacke
Simme, a drousie one, a lyngrer, a double dealer, a wanton, or a carelesse one,
among the reielles and wretches of
this worlde: that in their coldenesse,
darkenesse, hopelesse houeryng, vayne
deuising, wilfulnesse, tolitie, forgetfulnesse, contempte of God and Godlynesse, tempteth so hygh, so magnificent,
terrible & great God of maiestie, most
deadlily to danger them selues: who diuersly in a moment, and in the twin-
kling of an eye, is able by his iustice
to destroy thee, to cracke sodainely in
sun-

sunder the thred of thy life, & to twine
strõgly the cordes of thy perdurable &
eternal death. Therfore as he ought, in
his mightinesse, of euery wighte to be
feared: so he shold not of any one, either
presumptuously or vainely be tempted.
But for thy part, obey him in his will,
and suffer him with all pacience, to try
thee through aduersitie, cõmitting thy
selfe wholely vnto his oxly wil & mercy: for surely he will(beholding in thee
the power of faithe) not suffer thee to
be tempted aboue thy strengthe, or
yeelde thee so farre to fall, but with his
owne right hand, will raise thee quick-
ly vp againe. And I exhorte thee also to take heede, that thou possesse not
in his sight at any time, an vnstayed,
ofte wauering, and winde shaken hart,
through Sathans blustrings, stormie
and tempestuous blastes, stirred vppe
daily and hourely againste thee, and
that by Goddes permission for good:

least by thine impaciencie, diffidente
trembling, and sore shakes of thine vn-
chriſten inconſtancie, thou be ſodainly
turned to thy ſhiftes, put to thy faultie
flight, and ſo be diſpoſſeſſed of thy verie
healthful, ſafe, and moſt ſure holde : or
elſe ſpoiled with reproche of thy chriſten armor: or be occaſioned by deſpe-
rate purſute, to ſtarte from the face of
the enimie, to ſtacker fearfully at his
offered blowes, and in hazarde to take
hurt by ſome dangerous and ſodain fal.
greatly to diſhonor thee before Chriſte
thy captaine : and with him infinite
armies of heauēly ſoldiors: whoſe tents
(to encourage thee)are pitched round
about thee. I ſay therefore vnto thee
(O Chriſtian)ſtand thou cherefully to
thy charge in all things , and defende
mãfully thine owne : diſmaiſ thee not
I ſay : for the Lorde God him ſelfe
will be thy defender and keeper , and
wil ſtand by thee to ſtrengthen thee,
and

to the Reader.

and to deliuer thee from all daungers.
And if legions of diuels should cōpasse
thee, trench thee in round about, plant
their power, and bēd forcibly their shot
agaynst thee: Well may they threat-
ningly thunder far frō thee, rore, rattle
and rumble in the aire ouer thee, tum-
ble terribly about thee, parche some-
thing thy tender skin, and wonderfully
in such sort amase thee: yet shall they
not preuayle agaynst thee, hurte any
member of thee, or once remoue thy fast
fixed foote, but shalt stād sure for euer,
euen as the highe, mightie, steadie, and
strong mounte Sion: for Gods arme
stayeth thee, who by his power hathe
ouercome the diuell, euen the great diuell Sathanas him selfe, he holdeth him
at will by his infernall chaynes, his
whole cursed armie also, hell gates, and
al the powers of hell. O praise therfore
thine almightie God: exalt his glorious
name for euermore, watche and pray

*** v.   con-

continually: pray with vnderstãding,
pray at al times, and in al places, as his
holy spirite shall moue thee, for the vp-
holding of thee, and for the auoyding
of the engins, sleights, and tẽptations of
the enimies : that God himselfe may be
pleased, thy soule strēgthned, the diuels
chased, vãquished, or put to flight. And
when thou prayest, deceiue not vaynly
thy selfe: be not blinded with the proud
Pharisie in thine owne conceite, boa-
sting of thy righteousnesse in the presence of God, neither glorying in any
thing: for he throughly beholdeth thee,
and seeth that truely in thee, euen thy
secrete and hidde sinnes (a masse of all
abhomination) as thou oughtest chie-
fly therein to be thine owne iudge. But
humble thy self before him, with the penitent and poore wretched Publicane,
confessing thy sinnes and wickednesse:
and feare not then to attayne grace,
through suche true faith & hũblenesse.

M ore.

Moreouer, forget not, that as God is a moste highe, heauenly and diuine sub-stance, and a spirite of al goodnesse and truth: so wil he also of thee be spiritually worshipped, praysed, and prayed vnto, euē in the truth, by the word of truth, and frō the depth and botome of thine hart. This also I put thee in remēbrāce of (a thing greatly requisite) that in the tyme of thy prayers, which thou daily consecratest to god (be they more or lesse, long or short) thou be not with-drawen with the snarling suggestions, secret twitches, inward motions, or wy-lie sleightes of the enimie Sathan, tho-rough the abuse of thy senses and out-warde bodily members, as thine eyes, thine eares, and suche like: that whi-lest thy tongue onely oft babbleth, and vaynely wastest muche breath: thine hearte, whiche God chiefely respe-cteth, and dothe very gladly desire, bee fardest off, and bee moste vaynely

turned

turned another way, gretly to displeast
him, to vexe sore thine owne conscience,
and to make vtterly frustrate al thine
attempts, or importune sutes of greate
necessitie. This I say also vnto thee: If
thou desire to be the child of God, and
voyde of al doubts so in dede to be, sa-
uour frō thy hart Christ thy forerun-
ner and sauiour, by whose onely grace
thou arte adopted the childe of God.
Make not towards him, thy fidelitie,
crased, mingled, or patched: let it goe
soundly and al whole togither, both frō
thy body & thy soule. Let him alwayes
enioy frō thee the whole & perfect mā,
the man regenerate & new borne, and
made by his spirst the child of light, ful
of agilitie and liuelinesse: whose soule
mounting with felicitie still vp to the
heauens, is there resident with Chryst
the sauiour, and alwayes conuersant in
heauenly things. And let him also bee
euermore vnto thee, thine onely, whole,
full,

ful, perfect, and sufficient redemer, ear
nest petitioner and ready pacifier of
the diuine fury against thee for al can-
ses. who with great glory (as thou shol-
dest confisse) is ascended on high, and
sitteth with almightinesse, power and
maiestie, on the right hand of his heauenly father, with open and fresh blee-
ding wounds (the manyfest marks &
impressions before him for euer) of the
purchasd & most preciouse redeemed
inheritance, euen for thee, most notori-
ouse and deadly sinner, by the secrete
testimonie of thine owne conscience.
These things & such like, of thee thus
christenly considered, thou mayest bee
bold with thy most merciful and louing
God. But yet agayne I say vnto thee,
hold thee sure vnto thy sauiour christ,
swarue not frō him, nor frō the vertue
of his onely merites, wherby thou must
be onely saued. Cleaue then close to the
rocke of assurance: leane to no loose nor
                                    sandie

sandie safetie. Trust not to the rotten-
nesse of our humane deuises, labour not
to languish in a maze of vncertaintie.
Bemoyle not thy selfe in suche myre of
mortalitie, and shun soone such shoures
as wil wrecke thy soules fidelitie. Then
cry (as I sayd) and ceasse not to crane
pardon of God thy father in his sonne:
name, Doubte not of thy suite, what so
euer it be, for it shal by good motio be so
vpright, so reasonable, so acceptable before him and allowable: and shal touch
therwith so neere the tendernesse of his
mercy, his truthe and fidelitie, that of
necessitie graunt muste bee made vnto
thee: he wil not denie thee the requests
of thy lippes : yea, he will so graciously
tender thee, that foreseing thy cause of
inwarde complaynte, he wyll prepare quickely thine heart most faithfully to call vpon him. Beleeue therfore
faithfully, trust of assurance, and thou
shalte surely obteine thy desire, with
great

greate mercy and fauour at his holy
hande. Thy sinnes shal not be imputed
vnto thee, thou shalte bee blessed and
righteouse in the sighte of God all the
dayes of thy life, so happily shall thine
hart be prepared: so mightily shal thy
prayers preuayle for thee: they will
forcibly pearce the celestiall and high
heauens: approche neare to the onely throne of grace and maiestie: cry
incessantly for thee, & will not returne
from the presence of God, nor once be
satisfied, before the full graunt of their
humble sute, for thy sauing healtb and
comoditie. To conclude in all thy godly attemptes, whether in praying, fasting, geuing of Almes, frequenting
the holy Sacramentes, or rendering
moste hartie thankes vnto God, for his
infinite *Mercies, Graces, Blessinges*
and *Benefites* bestowed vppon thee,
and vppon his whole *Churche,* from
the beginning vntill this present day:
and

and what soener in holinesse thou com-
mendest daily vnto him: let it always
be done vprightly, orderly, with christian comelynesse, and modestie, with
peace of conscience, faithfully, constantly, cherefully, and in charity, as the only worde of God moste strautely byn-
deth thee. Which I pray to God may
clerely shine into thee by the power of
his holy spirite: who quicken thee this
day, to morow, and for euer, and kindle in thee towardes him, the firie
flames of his true loue, throughe his
sonne Chryst Iesus: who speedely
graunt thee the same signement
of his holy hand, and satis-
fie thee with inward
ioy, in all thy
moste lowefull and diuine
desires. Amen.

(∴)

FINIS.

A deuout meditation

of the godly Christian, with a
briefe Confession and Prayer.

When I (O heauen-
ly father) thozowe
the glozie of thine
only eternal grace
am cuē in the mid-
dest of many mu-
ses, lamentable mournings, deepe
sighings, and inwarde monings to
my self, most happily stirred to the
due consideration of my self, and in
what perillous state I euer stande
here in this wretched worlde, how
in the breuity therof I am compassed with many miseries, with gre-
uous plagues and punishmentes,
with dreadful calamities, perilles,
and dangers, with diuers maladies
sicknesses aand infirmities bothe of

A.j.   body

The mercy & grace of God in the hearts of his elect, to cosider in this life their dangerous and miserable state for sinne.

body and mind: how by the mighty power also & pollicie of mine ancient and most deadly enimy the olde subtile serpent, this deceitful vaine world, as also mine own weaknes, corruption, apte inclination, & most vile subiection to sinne, J am daily assaulted and tempted to sinne, and in committing sinne, become the seruant of Sin, & must acordingly looke for death the iuste reward of sinne : bicause diuersly therwith and damnably (through disobedience & the breach of thy law, in thought, word and deede) J haue and do most greuously offend the will of thy Maiestie, and am become thereby a very Sathanist, the childe of the diuel, to hasten thy furies vpon mee, that he shuld vse his tiranie against me (for so witnesseth by accusation my wounded conscience,) wherby my soule is daylie dysquieted, sore clog-

clogged, gretly defiled, maruelously amased, made monstruouse before thee, and hated of thee : whereunto (my freedom and innocencie being lost) of my owne concupiscence am accustomably blinded, drawne and entised : and by the malice thereof, both vnderstanding, heart and wil are holden captiue and in deadelie slauery to the diuel, the only author and beginner of all euell concupiscence and sinne. By which occasiō, in stead of healthsome and profitable thinges, I ofte desire very noysome, most pernitious and hurtfull things. And my soule also which in the excellencie therof, through reason and the vprightnesse of the inward man, should beare the beauty of thy heauenly and most glorious ymage in perfect puritie and innocencie, through the corruption therof is fowly deformed and sore ble-

A.y. nished,

Cōcupiscence and the malice therof.

The diuell the onely author of concupiscence and sin.

*The soules de-
formitie tho-
rowe sinne.*

*True faith in
the abounding
mercies of
God.*

mished, and made accordingly his
euill fauoured & most filthy image,
and so worthily by thy iustice shaken off, and caste from the presence
of thy deitie. So that hæreby (O
Lord) thou hast yet by the continuance of thy grace moued me to consider, that if thy mercies did not a-
bounde vppon me, or that thy gratious fauoure, should nowe or at any
time, in this most deadly plight vtterly forsake me, and not rather cō-
fortably with spæedy and most swift
sway turne againe towardes me,
and bring therwith from thine heauenly presence, the distilling moy-
stures, and large flowing streames
of thy celestiall dewe, plentifully
drawne from the swæte fountains
of my sauiour'e, to refresh, comfort,
make whole againe, clense & beau-
tifie, my very leprous, moste sinneful and sicke soule, and of thy mære
mercie,

mercie to reduce hir to hir priſti-
nate & former ſtate : my caſe ſhould
be moſt miſerable, my bands ſhuld
be indiſſoluble, I ſhoulde become a
curſed reied, & remain a fire brand
of hell for euer. But as thy loue (O
Lord) is vnſpeakeable, and thy fatherly mercie toward me infinite,
which willeſt not the deathe of a
ſinner, but rather he ſhould tourne
from his wickedneſſe and liue, and
offreſt him time and ſpace to repēt
and amende : ſo haſte thou now in
mercie remembred me, loked back
againe vpon me, cheared and comforted me, encreaſed true faithe in
me, thy ſpirit hath renued me, ſtirred me to call moſte humbly vnto
thée, ſet me frée from the ennemie,
pitied my ſoules deformitie, prepared the moſt healthful remedie : for
the bloud of thy ſonne Ieſus hathe
clenſed me, whereby thou haſte ſo

The miſerable
ſtate of the
ſicke ſoule,
without true
faith in the fre
mercy of god.

The feeling
of the grace
of god.

quickened me, that my soule reioy-
seth within me, with most earnest
teares it repenteth me that euer I
sinned against thée, I fall flat to the
earthe before thée, confessing my
sinnes vnfainedly, my weakenesse
and infirmitie, for I haue most greuously offended thée, my conscience
therein accuseth me, & crie yet with
true faithe vnto thée: Mercie good
Lord mercie, with thankes giuing
and extolling thée, for thine infused
grace vppon me. And I pray thée
moste humblie (O my God of all
mercie) to continue thy fatherly affection, the encreasing of thy grace,
and strength of thy spirit vpon me,
to helpe, to directe and comfort me,
vnto the ende, and in the ende in all
my temptations, troubles, weakenesse and infirmities bothe of bodie
and minde: Least sathan (as I said)
preuaile and confound me, the tick-
ling

The humble submission & confession of the faythfull soule.

A calling vn- to God for comfort and strength.

ling pleasures of this world deceiue me, and the olde man my wretched flesh, which is not yet subiect to the spirite, do master me: against all which, I must arme my self, stande to the battaile, continually fighte, holde out at the swordes pointe, offer the pricke, driue backe, chase, ouerthrowe, wound and confounde, whilest breath shall holde in this wretched body:yea, I say wretched in dæde, being compassed with so many calamities and infinite miseries:for the which cause, (O Lord) I craue alwayes thy mightie power, in my weakenesse I make my mone, haste thæ nowe to helpe me, O strengthen me, graunte me thy presence, stande by me, encourage me to fight manfully,that by thæ I may amaze the enemies, put them fast to flight, gette the victorie, triumphe before thæ, and extoll thæ

in

A.iiij.

The sighte of the faythfull soule.

in thy great might & mercie, nowe and foz euer:thzough Iesus Chzist our Lozd : who liueth and raigneth with thée and the holy Ghost in all honoure and glozy wozlde without ende. Amen.

I I.

To dwell in the seruice of God, to haue the world, and the pleasures there-of in cõtempt, and ro striue daily against them with the armor of rightuousnesse.

Oz as muche (O almightie God) as we are all warned by thine holye Apostle Iohn, not to bée louers of thys euyll wozld,noz the bain pleasures ther-of, bicause bothe the one and the o-ther come vtterly to naughte : and that also to be a louer of the wozld,
is

is to be an hater of thée, to slip from thy will, and from the presence of thy maiestie, as one that regardeth thée not, knowes thée not, neither séeke to know thée, but startle aside from thée, forsaketh the right way, and entreth of will the perrillous way full of hidde thistles, thornes, briers, brambles, venemous wormes and serpentes: linking also the selues into the amitie, league and seruice, of the moste sleightie, hatefull and deadly enemie, the proude Prince of this worlde, who for a time by Gods permission is broke lose, and rageth in his course, roareth and fighteth continually against the Soule of man: who entangleth only his owne to their vtter ouerthrowe, with the vaine pleasures thereof: euen with the delightes in effect but of one houre, and with the encreasing of sorowes for manye

A.v.   yeares:

What danger hey fall into that forsake god, and leane to the worlde and the pleasures thereof.

The seruice of God, what it is.

yéeres: I beséeche thée (O thou king of all holinesse) whose seruice is most highe, most happie, most sure, most healthfull, wealthful, heauenly, perpetuall, perfecte felicitie and frædome :) which séest the weakenesse, inconstancie, greate miserie, and necessitie of me thine humble seruaunt: the outrage also & power of my cruel aduersaries: graunt me sufficiencie of thy grace, & strengthe of thine holy spirite, that by vertue thereof, I may be directed in ƴ way wherin I should walke, my pathes made straite, and my fœte stedfast, alwayes to withstande the euil attemptes of the moste wicked, and the outwarde glittering glozes of this sinful and vain world, and not yéelde my minde to the pleasures & comfortes of the same, as a childe of vanitie, enclosed therin for ƴ time, as in a déepe dungeon of daunger,

and

and of deadly darkenesse, founded vppon a sandie and rotten soile, very olde, ruinous, sore shaken, and readie at euery momente to fall, throughe age vppon me : but to be otherwise staide by thine holy and mightye arme, pacientlie in the meane season to abide thy will, to lay my foundation sure, to be sober and watchfull ouer all daungers, to stretch forth mine handes to the battaile, to strengthen mine armes like a bow of steele, that vnder thy protection & power, I may manfully resist all hurtful euilles, and the assaults of the wicked, and stand stably to my profession in thy holy seruice, wherunto thorow thy grace I am called, to the ende, that by thine only helpe, I should do the workes of rightuousnesse. O thou rightuous Lorde and God of my strengthe, which haste made me,

the worlde, a deepe dongeon, wherin the children of vanitie are enclosed.

which

which haſt conſerued me, and arte
moſte louing and carefull ouer me,
I putting mine only hope and confidence (not in the holy Angels, celeſtiall ſpirites, bleſſed Sainctes in
heauen, oꝛ good men hǽre in earth)
but only in thǽ,ſuffer me not to be
tempted aboue my ſtrengthe, oꝛ to
be ouerwhelmed of mine owne cõ-
cupiſcéce:but in the midſt of temptation, make thou a way foꝛ me to
eſcape with ioy. Thou(O God)art
only omnipotent, moſte gratious,
ful of al goodneſſe,faithfulneſſe and
truthe:fulfil therfoꝛe thy pꝛomiſſes
towardes me,moſt merciful Loꝛd,
thou God of truthe:Put vppon me
thine whole armoꝛ of rightuouſe-
neſſe, O thou God of mighte and
true holineſſe, that by thy power I
may be ſtrong againſt all aduerſa-
ries:foꝛ I wꝛeſtle not(as thou knoweſt) againſt fleſh and blud in this
life:

Armoure of
rightuouſ-
neſſe.

life : but against rule, against power, and againste worldly rulers of the darknesse of this worlde, and againste spirituall wickednesse in heauenly things : by whome, without thine heauenly power I stande euer in hazarde to eternall destruction bothe of body and soule. For which cause (I say) O my swate God, arme me strongly, strengthen me in my weakenesse, and make me stoute, that in this christen chiualrie, I may stand perfecte in all things before thee, and not slippe by cowardise or inconstancie from thy faithful seruice: but fight vnder thy banner vntil the last breath, couragiously putting mine enemyes to flight, and cary away with triumph, a glorious victorie ouer them. So shall it come to passe, that thorowly running this so shorte a race in my holy calling as a puissant warrior

Christian chiualrie.

The fight of a christien souldioure in the seruice of god must be continuall and couragious.

rior in thy most high and excellent
seruice, with lawfull striuing, and
with violent plucking towards me
thine heauenly kingdome, I shall
in the ende perfectly sée it and possesse it, and shall receiue in mine
handes a Palme of victorie, vppon
mine head, a Crowne of glory prepared, the hidde Manna also and a
white stone, wherein is written a
newe name, which no man knoweth, sauing only the receiuer of it :
who shal serue thée thou great God
of heauen, in the moste sacred state
of true holinesse, perfecte frædome,
excellencie, dignitie, and equalitie
with thine holy Angels and al blessed Saincts, in euerlasting felicitie.
Graunt this mine humble petition
(O Lorde) for thy greate mercies
sake : So shall I here, and in eternall blessednesse, extoll and magnifie thy glorious name. Amen.

For

Palme of vi-
ctorie.
Crowne of
glorie.
Hid Manna.
And a White
stone.

111.

For the humble hearing, apte recei
uing, keeping, and continuing of the
vvoorde of God amongſt vs.

Onſidering (o thou
God of al holineſſe)
that the certainetie
of oure Chriſtian
faithe, ſtandeth by
the Scriptures or immoueable
woorde of thy truthe: which, as thy
meſſenger proceedeth from thee by
thy gratious inſpiration or ſecreate
brething: wherunto, as vnto a feaſt
royal, euery man of al nations vnder heauen are called: but are of thy
Church only receiued and deuoutly
vſed, to the inſtruction, cenfirmati-
on, ſtrengthening and eſtabliſhing
of thine only faithfull & true flocke:
and be, as thy bleſſed Apoſtle calleth them, ſacred and holy : bicauſe
they be heauenly, moſte pretious,
diuine,

the ſcriptures
of God, only
receyued of
the faithfull.

diuine, healthfull, and comfortable
to the soule, excelling all the wise-
dom of Philosophers, and the vainly wise of this world, and be therefore (in their high power and maiestie) worthily aboue all aduanced,
segregate, and put aparte by them
selues, from all other wrytings of
prophane matters and the flitting
descriptions of men: not onely per-
taining to this present worlde, and
for the vse of this temporal life: but
also from all Ethnicke superstitions, false worshippings, wicked sa-
crifices and erronious opinions, v-
sed contrary to thy word, & against
thée the only eternal and true God:
which, by lying, custome and crueltie, are corruptly crepte into thy
Church, to the foule féeding, filling,
defiling, and poisonning therof, and
is yet daily occasioned therby wout
thy grace, to be sinisterly drawne
and

Superstitions, false worshippings. &c.

and seduced, straying frõ the right way, and haled to death by will in oure selues, from the life that is in thee, euen to eternall death and destruction: we beseeche thee moste humbly (O thou gracious God) to enspire vs with thy holy spirite of truthe, ꝛ to kindle in all our hartes the fire of thy loue, light and truth: that by thy power in them, oure faithes may be strengthened, oure soules also humbled, rightly ledde and instructed, in thy word of loue, light, truthe, and of eternall life: by vertue wherof, at our first entrãce to Christ our high Pastor, we may truely vnderstande our profession and promisse in holy baptisme, and haue it accordingly wryften with thy finger of grace in our hartes, to the true knowledge of thy law, and the spiritual vnderstanding therof, to loue thee moste wꝛthily aboue

Our professiõ in holy Baptisme.

all,

B.j.

all, and our neighbor as our selues:
as also to knowe the promisses of
thy mercie in thy sonne oure Sauiour Iesus Christ most soundly and
purely, as thy holy word expresseth
therein: whereby we may be well
vpholden, and zealously staide in
our profession, to treade our pathes
right, to be guided by the true light,
to heare gladly the voice of oure
shepheard Iesus Christe, to testifie
his name, to folowe him the onely
true lighte, and not to feare the powers of darknesse, but to ouercome
them by thy mighte (although euen
with the losse of our liues) not only
the dalyings, dimme deuises and
vanities of the wicked, and to shun
all suche hatefull enemies, as are
vsuall mockers, daily depzauers,
sinnefull despisers, wilfull impug-
ners, wicked seducers, double dea-
lers, backe sliders, & pluckers back
from

Enemies of
Gods word.

from thy word, but also the sleights
of their father Sathan, the entice-
ments of the worlde, and the filthie
motions of the fleshe. And to that
happie ende (O Lorde) we may be
constant, and thy worde euer abide
in vs, Stirre vs vp to continuall and
hartie prayer, quicken our zeale, &
worke in vs, a true, liuely, quicke,
and frutefull faithe : that it being a
bright shining light in our hartes,
to the expelling of all Hipocrisie,
cloudinesse, darknesse and erroure,
and also our conuersation being answerable to our profession, the continuance of thy grace may stil comfortably shine vppon vs, thy holy
worde may continue amongste vs,
may be truely preached vnto vs, diligently, boldly, and zealously vtte-
red ouer al, and by al the ministers
thereof, by what occasion, time and
place so euer it be : for vnto vs that

B.y.   shall

Hartie prayer
to God, ma
keth vs con
stante in the
word of God.

The worde of God, what it is, and how of the godly to be confidred.

shall be saued, it is a thing moste precious and holy: It is the worde of life, the worde of reconciliation, the lanterne vnto oure féete, and a light vnto our pathes, the fountaine of wisedome, the breade of life, the foode of the soule, thy mightie power, and sworde of the spirite. And for as much (O heauenly father) as thy wordes thus to vswarde (come from heauen) are spirite and life, and are not to be wayed with the vaine imagination, policie, wisedome or witte of man, nor yet to be applied vnto the hurtfull pleasures of this sinnefull worlde, but to be moste holily and highly estéemed, moste humbly had in credite, reuerently thought vppon, gladly inclined vnto, heard with silence, and receiued with all modestie & ghostly gréedinesse: we humbly beséeche thée, that as thou haste euer héeretofore

fore ben the only gratious director, instructor and teacher of thy holy Patriarks and Prophets, Apostles and holy fathers from time to time from the beginning, and amongst al men (for thine electes sake in Iesus Christe) continuest yet so still vntill this day: O traine vs vp also in thine heauenly knowledge we pray thee: prepare our harts, teach vs thy law, and wryte thy woordes of life in the tables of oure heartes: that in these our monstrous dayes of moste wilfull vanitie, which in their strangenesse crieth oute (by plagues) to be punished, we may aforehande be warned, we may be yet better schooled, thy wrath thereby preuented, our soules more spiritually nourished, filled with thy fauoure, more mortified daily from the vanities of this brickel life, guided to more christian modestie and

B.iij. tem-

God the only instructour of all, in all ages.

An apt Prayer for these oure dayes.

temperãce, affected solie to the way
of holinesse, comforted in all troubles and aduersities, boldned manfully against the face of ye enemies,
stayed, well armed and strengthened against all temptations, stirred
vp to the encrease of all vertues:
that thy woordes (which shal iudge
vs in the last day) being by thy ministers truely preached, and of vs
also as zealously embraced, and by
any meanes not to be despised or
slandered, but on all partes surely
holden, and to shewe forthe accordingly the true frutes of rightuousnesse, we may be called of thée, thy
holy disciples, & auoide I say the fal
of thy vēgeãce amōgst vs, thy iudge
ment also to eternal condemnation
& be receiued in time to euerlasting
saluation: throughe thy grace & the
only merites of thy sonne our Lord
Iesus Christ. Amen.

For

IIII.

For Fayth.

B reading or hearing thy holy worde (O blessed sauiour) we are taught, that true fayth which is thine onely gifte, is onely therby attayned : and that by the power of thine heauenly spirite it is breathed into the onely hearts of all thine electe, who receiue it by measure and quantitie according to the will and power of the same spirite : and with thine eyes beholding it in them, thou gloriest in them, thou daily blessest them, thou encreasest it in them, thy countenance shineth vppon them, thou amiably appearest and shewest thy selfe vnto them : yea so acceptable it is in

B.iiij.   thy

Diuine Meditations.

Faithe only breathed into the hartes of Gods elect.

thy sighte (O sweete sauiour) that thou bæing the king of eternall glory and maiestie, art espoused to the soules of the faithfull, and makest them thereby to be partakers with thæ of thine heauenly and diuine nature, through the wonderful operation of thine holy spirite. We are taught by thine holy Apostle, that what so euer is not of this faith, is sinne, and that there is no possibilitie without it to please thæ, or to finde grace by sute at thyne holy hande. And therefore all they that

True faithe in Chrilte.

come vnto thæ, must in dæde firmly beleæue, that thou art very God and very Man : yea, and suche a God of mighte, of mildenesse & great mercy aboue all Gods, as both can and euer will heare, incline thine eare, and abundantly rewarde all them, that with liuely and true faith seke thæ, and vnfaignedly desire to finde thæ, thée, oz to be relieued by thine holy hande. By this fayth (O Lozde) we also obteine of God thy father, all good things : yea, what so euer we craue at his hande in thy name. Through this fayth also, so many as beléeue are iuſtified, made the ſonnes and heires of God, and enioy moſt certainly thereby the rewarde of euerlaſting life. O Lozde Ieſu, great is the power and wozking of this fayth, foz by it the conſciences of the godly are quieted, by it they truely know thée the onely high and eternall God : by it they loue and feare thée, be conſtant towards thée, ſtrong and pacient in al aduerſitie, their hope is firme foz things to come : by it they conceiue boldeneſſe to repaire to the thzone of thy grace foz mercy, to haue ſure truſt in thée, to inuocate thine holy name, to adoze and wozſhippe it, to

Faithe iuſti-ficth.

The power of Faith.

B. v.   confeſſe

confesse the truthe before thée, to obey it moste gladly, to perseuer therein moste willingly, to withstande the force of all tyrannie, to yéelde vp in time their spirite, and to goe through fayth to thine and their heauenly father. Séeing then (O graciouse God and Sauiour) that this vertue is so heauenly, so holy, so mightie, so acceptable and preciouse in thy sight, that without it nothing can be well pleasing the will of thy maiestie, or to serue happily our owne turnes : and we also of suche frailtie can not attayne to this moste singuler treasure, except it come from aboue (euen from thée) and infused into our hearts by the grace of thine holy spirite : we moste hartily beséeche thée (by the power thereof) to make cleane our hearts, to purge them of all error, darknesse, and ignorance, of all mistrust,

truſt, infidelitie, and vnfaythful-
neſſe, and to plant moſte ſpædely in
vs, a true, liuely, and vndoubted
faithe, in the bleſſed and moſte glorious Trinitie: in God our heauenly father, in thæ (O God) oure only
ſauioure, and in the holy ghoſte our
moſt deare and ſwæte comfoztour:
by whome alone, we be all highly
bleſſed, pzeciouſly redæmed, and
eternally ſanctified : and that alſo
foz thine only ſake (O bleſſed ſauioure) thine heauenly father is well
pleaſed with vs, our ſinnes clærely
remitted vnto vs. This faithe (O
ſwæte Ieſu) daily encreaſe in vs,
help moſt gratiouſly our vnbelæfe,
O Lozd ſtrengthen vs from faithe
to faithe : that we may at the laſte
thozow thine accuſtomed grace, be
made perfectly faithfull, conſtante
warriozs, and valiant conqueroz,
in the defence of thine holy religiõ,
                                    againſt

againſte the power of Sathan, the worlde, and Antichriſte: and in all things to ſhewe oure ſelues in this life, bothe in our profeſſion & manners, truly and frutefully faithful, euen to the high exaltation & praiſe of thy name: which liueſt and raigneſt, with God the father, and God the holy Ghoſte, true and perfecte God, our onely mediator and aduocate, world without end. Amen.

v.

To the attainement of Grace, and for the due examination of ſuche deſires and motions, as are put daily into oure mindes.

Bholding (O God our maker) the miſerable ſtate of mãkinde in this lyfe, how diuerſly therein and in ſinitely he is

is continually beset, compassed and hedged in with bodily and ghostly euil, stepping euery moment amõg the low shrubbes, lurking stubbes, stumbling blockes, craggie rockes, dead pits, trappes, catches, snares, grinnes, furious and fierse beastes, in the wildernesse of this worlde to present destruction: alwayes vncertaine and feareful through danger, whereunto (in his wayes) he may leane or trust, wandring in this desert among doutful chaunces, voide of certain hope, farre off from comfort, forsaken of frendes, beset with many enemies, and entised diuersly to sundry desires and motions, & so moste grcenously perplexed, and inwardly afflicted in minde, musing before thee (O Lorde) in thine heauenly presence, vpon hys moste wretched state, what shall betide him, knoweth not what to doe,
which

The miserable state of man in thys life.

Man posses
seth in himself
two powers,
and of sundry
inclinations.

which way to turne him, whether
to flee, not certaine of his ende, ignorant, when, howe, and where he
shall ende his dayes, and leaue to
earthe his moste wretched and
earthie carcasse: who during his
shorte time, possesseth two powers,
diuersly drawing and leading him:
althoughe onely one preuayleth,
either with him or against him,
which is, a willyng consente to
vayne pleasures bredde in the
corrupted flesshe: or otherwise, a
more apte inclination to the good
wil and motion of the spirit, which
are bothe contrary the one to the o-
ther, and the one continually war-
ring or waging battaile against the
other: whose fight (if there be resi-
stance) are bothe very violente to
preuaile, & stirreth daily the soule
to great vnrest. Which powers or
partes of man (O Lord) in the time
of

of innocencie, befoze the fall of my first parents, haddest coupled them togither in moste blessed concozde and vnitie, but (alasse) nowe separated, peace bzoken and set at discozde, by the Serpente the enemie of peace and of mankinde: and cannot liue ioyned togither, wythoute contynuall warre, ruffeling and wzangling together as things dyuers, althoughe in dæde but one: J besæche thæ therefoze (O my God the greate God and maker of heauen and earthe) to beholde with greate compassion, my miserable state among the rest in this moste wofull and grævous conflicte, my greate frailetie and weakenesse wythoute thy grace, my darknesse and ignozaunce, and the power of sinne raygning in myne earthely and moztall members: that as thou arte God the authoz of peace, the

The serpent cause of discorde.

the true light and guid, and the only God of my strengthe, to preuaile
for me by thine holy spirit, against
the Prince of sedition and darkenesse, of fraud and deceit, of erroure
and lies, and the corrupted motions
of the sinneful flesshe : so graunt me
the strengthe of thy grace, a liuely
and quicke féeling faithe also in thy
promisses thorowe Christe : that
thereby my spirite being alwayes
prepared, quickned and directed by
thy spirite, it may yélde to the only
quickening and good motions therof : that by the heauenly power of
it, I may at all times be constante
in them, and learn perfectly by due
examination, and with good desires
out of thy worde of truth, the euent
of all attemptes, stirres, motions,
assaultes, entisements, desires, prouocations and affections, to iudge
truely of them, to way rightly their
natures,

Prince of
sedition.

The meane to
knowe the
good motions
from the bad.

natures, from whence they come, by what spirite, to what ende, whether worthy thy well liking, tending to thy glory, answerable to my profession, making for the peace of my conscience or to the contrary: and so by due triall to forsake the one and embrace the other : least throughe lewde carelessenesse, or not aptly yelding to the good motions of thine holy wil, I giue thine offered grace moste gracelesly the slippe : becomming in thy sighte but a fugitiue, a roage, a runneagate, a corner creeper, a vaine dullarde, grose, earthie, lumpishe and heauie, voide of spirit and life, darke in true iudgemente, affected to vaine desires, moste wickedly falling from thee, forsaken also of thee, giuen ouer to my selfe, wretchedly wandring at will or at the wilde aduenture, and stande as a dead pray to the will of al deuou-

C. j. ring

The inconuenience of carelesnesse, or not to receiue in time the good motions of God.

ring aduersaries: euen to ẏ sleights of the moste cursed serpente, to the sugred baits of this deceitful world, and to the filthie desires of the rebellious fleshe: by whome I shal be most wickedly seduced, moste horribly blinded and fowly corrupted: and so trained on in a short race to the slaughter, euen to the swalowing gulffe of despaire, the bottomelesse hurlepoole, or most deepe sinke of destruction. O my god of al mercie and grace, that art the only helper of me in all my necessities, assist and comfort my soule with thy spirite of lighte and truthe : that I may nowe and at all times bothe truely discerne, retaine wyth good will, and folow, the only good motions thereof, and forcibly withstãd the contrary: that no prouocations, venemous enticementes, or poysoned pleasures of the fleshe, be occasions

The power of the spirite of light and truthe.

sions to defile and hazard my soule.
But folowing the good desires of the
spirite (which are moste pure, perfect and godly,) and my soule euer
mindefull of hir celestiall nature,
enforsing hir selfe vpwarde to the
high heauens before thy presence:
there may spring vp vnto me (all
the dayes of my life) the good continuance of thy grace, the blessed trã-
quillitie of an innocent minde, the
reaped frutes also of a good spirite,
and lastly in time euerlasting life,
which thou hast prepared for me
thorow thine only mercy and
grace, in the merites of
thy sonne and my sa-
uior Iesus Christ.
Amen.

C.ij.   For

V I.

For the chastising of the Soule, to keepe it lowe and in subiection.

The way and mene to plese God in this life.

WE be taught of thee (O thou GOD of heauen) that who so euer wil rightly prosper in this life, and goe daily forwardes in true godlynesse woorthy thy wel liking, must tast substantially of thine heauenly wisedome, and enter the way thereto with all lowly subiection, holding still faste thy reuerent feare, esteeming vnfainedly the way of thy testimonies, and be alwayes very watchful, that he offend not thy sight. It behoueth vs therfore (O Lord) in the state of our great weakenesse and frailetie, and in our darknesse and deadly ignorance,

noꝛance, to haue daily acceſſe to thee
(thou God of our power, true light
and wiſedome) by pꝛayer and moſt
humble ſute, that we may ſéeke by
thine heauenly wiſedome to know
thee truly, and to haue thy feare befoꝛe our eyes: that in our pꝛofeſſion
we may be euer conſtante, pacient
and ſtrong in thée, auoiding thoꝛow
thy grace al careleſſe ſecuritie, wã-
dꝛing inconſtancie and ſlipperneſſe:
kéeping all our powers vnder thine
holy diſcipline, without repining oꝛ
murmuring, and not yéelde vp our
ſelues (accoꝛding to the will of the
fleſhe) to flying vanities, and the
ſwifte flitting things of this woꝛld:
but cleaue ſtedfaſtly vnto thée, and
giue ouer our ſelues wholely, paciently to abide thy holy will, to the
quickning of vs in our dulneſſe and
humaine fearefulneſſe, and to the
ſwéete chaſtening of our vntoward

Holy diſci-
pline.

C.iij.   and

Exercises of the crosse.

and drousie soules. Doubtlesse (O Lord) very great, sweete & pleasant to the godly, is the commoditie of thy chastisements, and the exercises of thy crosse, to the encrease of godlinesse among thy children, and to suppresse the wil of the proud flesh: which, otherwise to the contrarie, would be soone ouerwhelmed with too much pride, iolitie, forgetfulnes, slouth and carelessenesse. Quicken vs therfore (O Lord) with the rod of thy fauoure, visite at times oure gracelesse dulnesse: ŷ we may feele thereby the touche of thy grace, the sorowes also of our mindes in oure offences, and cal our own wayes to remembrāce, that we may say with the holy Prophet: It is good for me Lord that I haue ben punished, and that to this happie ende, that I may learne thy statutes. Againe, before I was troubled, I went wrong. &c.

O

O graūt vnto vs most louing God, that with thy rod of fatherly corre-ction, we may iudge our selues hap-pie, ₵ reioyce with thy holy prophet least to the contrary, by sufferance ₵ euil custome, or hauing our reane of wantonnesse too much at liberty, we too toomuch deceiue our selues, ₵ in our forgetfulnesse, laughe at our own wickednesse, whē rather most bitterly we should bewaile our sin-fulnesse, ₵ remēber therby the infi-nite dangers to the soule, howe it is compassed, suttlely deceiued, holden captiue ₵ thral to the diuel. And we must cōfesse vnto thœ (O our god) ÿ we stand not at any time in true li-bertie or ioy effectual in any thing, onlesse we possesse by thy spirite thy reuerent feare, ₵ that also ioyned w a peaceable ₵ quiet cōsciēce. O what a happines therfore is it to a mā, to cast frœly frō him, al impedimēts ₵

The inconue-nience that commeth by sufferance and euill custome.

C.iiij.	lettes

Diuine Meditations.

He is happie, that humbleth him selfe to discipline.

lettes of worldly vanities, & yeelde him self wholely vnder thine hand of discipline, and to the chastening of his soule. Graunt vs (O Lord) to be so happie, that we may daily renounce and put from vs, what so euer may staine & burthen our most tender, weake, and simple consciences. Graunt vnto vs in this worlde of warfare, strengthe of thy grace, that we may fighte the battaile of christian souldiours, and ouercome by custome, the vsuall supporter of all euil. Graunt vs grace (O mercifull Lorde) that we may stand stedfastly to our charge, yeelde with patience to thy will, and in all things to take straight view of our selues, and cheefely with our owne eyes to beholde well our selues, that in thy sight we be all well armed, and so alwayes preuent the warning of others, to the ouerthrow of the deadly aduer-

aduersarie. Graunt this (o heauenly father) with humblenesse of hart we beseeche thee, to the quickening and strengthening of oure soules in al temptations and chastisements: and stirre vp daily in them, thyne heauenly sparkes and sweete motions of comfort, to their moste happie reioysing, and to the exaltation of thy moste glorious name in this life, and in the euerlasting worlde to come: through thy son Christ our Lorde. Amen.

VII.

For pacience in aduersitie, and to remember that this worlde is but a place of perigrination, or passing forwardes vnto an other worlde.

When thou in mercie (O lord) beholdest thine own, & seest them among others

C.v. how

how hazardly vnto deadly dangers they daily offer them selues, raunging abrode at aduenture like loste sheepe, and readie to be torn of euery sauage and deuouring beast: thou by and by of thy fatherly and teder pitie, considerest their miserable state and condition, and how needefull it is for them to be soughte oute with diligence, to be brought home againe to the folde, or to be pinned in, fauourably pinched a while in some bare pasture, and sometime to be kept lowe with thy milde touch of calamities and aduersities, to abate their courages, and to let their liuely leapes and oute girdes: by meanes whereof, they be oft called againe, better to remember them selues, and whereby they may also haue thee the more in minde, and truely to knowe their owne state in this life, whereunto they are called,

Man in present danger. God at hand to deliuer.

Pynches to the proude flesh are somtime necessarie.

led, and to whose seruice, to walke
in the wayes of thy preceptes, to
kéepe them euer within their boūds
and that during their shorte race,
they liue hǽre but as exiles or as
Pilgrimes farre from theyr owne
home, not to liue hǽre in felicitie,
not to regarde the pleasures of thys
worlde, either yet to put theyr hope
and affiance in them, but to vse thē
without abuse (as by the way) : but
for their only necessities homward:
we moste humbly besǽche thǽ (O
thou father of all mercie) that thou
wilt daily renue thy compassion vpon vs, that thou wilt tēder vs in our
frailty, lustinesse & vain iolitie, that
in our offences thou wilt vō mercie
reforme vs, & not vtterly by thy iustice confound vs: but sǽke mildely
for vs, call vs gently home to thy
shǽpfold, with mercie embrace vs,
& kǽpe vs togither for euer in one,

in

Man for a
time is but an
exile from his
home, and a
pilgrime.

in the sweete vnitie, felowship and amitie of thy flocke. And if at any time, we shall henceforthe wander abrode and goe astray, wherby we shall offend thee, and iustly incurre thy most heauie wrath and displeasure: we craue yet at thine holy hãd to remember thy mercie, and so (in the time of correction) to temper it with thy iustice: that we thy children by adoption and grace, may largely tast in that respect, the comfortes of thy moste tender and fatherly goodnesse: that as we shal for oure disobedience and sinne, iustly fæle some parte of thy iustice, and haue therfore great cause of inward grǽfe and heauinesse, & occasioned daily to grone in our hartes for our spǽdie deliuerance from thy rodde of correction, and to attaine againe the bright countinance of thy fauor: so we may also in the meanetime, possesse

The Iustice of God and sinne are not clerely seuered in this life amõg the children of God.

poſſeſſe a liuely faith, ſhewe foꝛthe
the fruites of the ſame, pꝛay continually vnto thée, and beare paciently thy holy will wyth all thankful-
neſſe all the dayes of oure lyues:
thꝛough the only grace of the highe
paſtoꝛ and chéefe ſhepheard of oure
ſoules, thy ſonne our Loꝛd and only ſauiour Ieſus Chꝛiſte. Amen.

VIII.

To be humble in the ſighte of God.

My loꝛd God, which
arte mine only good-
neſſe, a God of great
Maieſtie, and to be
bleſſed foꝛ euer: I
moſte pooꝛe and wꝛetched ſinner,
moſte vile wooꝛme, duſt and aſhes:
and of all others moſte vnwooꝛthy
thy grace and ſauour: yet beholding
thy great mercie, thy truthe and fidelitie,

Man but a
worme, duſte,
and aſhes.

delitie, thy vsual and approued clemencie, towardes all humble and
penitent sinners: I among the rest,
(but a lumpe of earthe, and shaken
by thy power to dust in a momēt:)
doe prostrate my selfe vppon the
earthe, bewailing before thæ my
moste sinnefull state, crying with
the Prophet, peccaui,peccaui, and
with repentante teares call for thy
mercie.

O my GOD almightie and
my maker, which truely knowest
me thy creature euen as I am, and
searchest thorowly in me, the very
secretes of the heart and raines : If
I should in thy sight (being nothing
of my self) estæme any thing of my
self or else glory in any thing besids
thæ vnder the sunne, thou woldest
as thou mightest by due iustice a-
gainste me, woorthily reproue me
and condempne me with the rest,
as

as most baine and for naught. Yea, mine own sinnes would accuse me vnto thée, and my conscience very terribly crie oute against me: for I am before thée but a thing of naught, and my sinnes hast thou sealed vp against me, to the terrifying alwayes of me, and to incurre daily in my mind diuers incommodities & inward anguishes, to myne owne ouerthrow and côfusion. But humbling my selfe before thée (O my God) and estéeming of my selfe, as (in déede I am) but vile duste and ashes, and cast vtterly from me all estimation of my selfe, being pressed downe (as it were) to nothing: then I trust I shall obtain thy mercie, then shall I hope to possesse the happie peace, then shall I féele true ioy in my self: for thy presence shall be euen at hand, thy grace shall côfort me, thy good spirit shal quicken me,

Man moste vayne and naught.

Mans humble subiection before God, arrayneth the grace mercy and peace of God.

me, thy fauozable coumtinance shal
cheare me vp, and thine heauenly
lighte approche neare mine heart:
wherby it shall most blessedly hap-
pen, that where I haue heeretofoze
most bainly esteemed, but the least
thing of my selfe, the same very
vaine oz small estimation conceyued, shall sodenly consume and va-
nische to naught foz euer : and shall
thencefoozth by the hand of thy ma-
iostie, be so vndoz pzopped and graciously holden vp, that I shall neuer decline from due consideration
of my selfe, what I am of my selfe,
what I haue bene, by whom I haue
my being, and from whence I am
come: namely, of nothing, and from
nothing: and being so lefte vnto my
selfe, I shall be founde nothing, but
only as a shadow, oz meere infirmitie and weakenesse. Therefoze, I
most humbly beseeche thee (O thou
father

Man a thing
of nothing.

father of al mercy) the only affured
ftay of thine inheritance, which fe-
uerely chafeft away the baine glory of man, turne a little towardes
me, tender me in my weakeneffe,
and fhewe me the ftrengthe of thy
countenaunce, that immediatly in
thee I may be ftrong, and newely
chæred vp with inwarde and heauenly gladneffe: that being entred
into moft fodaine admiration with
my felfe, to fæ my felf in a momēt,
by thy fatherly embzacement, rai-
fed vp to heauen, which by myne
owne pzoneneffe and waighte of
finne, was befoze caryed downe to
hell, I may thanke thæ my mofte
fwæte and louing God, and pzayfe
thæ with an humble and mofte
lowly heart, with continual mode-
ftie, zealoufly, religioufly and godly, in thought, wozd and dæde: thorowe thy mercie and grace in thy

D.j.   fonne

fonne Iefus Chrifte all the dayes
of my life. Amen. Amen.

 $\cdot$ x.

Of true obedience and fubiection,
to fuche as be in authoritie, according
to the vvoorde of God.

It is better for
a man to obey,
than to leane
to his owne
fway.

Oz as much (O hea-
uenly father) as it is
rather auaileable for
men in this worlde;
to be in fubiection to
other, than to leane to
their owne only fway and leude li-
bertie: and fo, muche moze fafely to
obey, than to beare rule, and haue
all at commaundemente : with all
humbleneffe we befeeche thee , to
direce vs with thy fpirite of humilitie and lowelineffe , and to be alwayes in fubiection to authozitie,
accoz-

according to thy worde, by the rule of thine holy Apostle : not onely for feare, for necessitie, and therefore painefully : but rather of true loue, duetifully, moste gladly, and that for conscience sake:

For otherwise (O Lorde) wee slippe from our Christian profession, true obedience, and moste reuerente subiection, and attaine not the true libertie of minde, and the shewing of obedyence from the hearte, and for Goddes sake : but fall of will moste wickedly, and as bonde slaues, into the sinne of hatred, contempte, murmuring, grutching, conspiring, rebelling, and into innumerable suche like, as men being wholely giuen ouer to a wicked will, running headlong into all kinde of mischiefes : whereby we become as reiectes, and caste awayes from thy glorious fauoure:

D.y. wee

The inconuenience that commeth by disobediéce.

we purchase thy displeasure, thou detestest our treacheries, the curse of the people shall fall vpon vs, the spoile of the innocentes, and theyr bloud shed shall crie for vengeance against vs, our dayes shalbe shortned, our offspring and family ashamed, vtterly confounded, contemned, and for euer brought to naught. O gratious God, graunt therefore that we may euer regarde thy wil, be mindefull of thy statutes, feare thy iudgements, and consider with our selues, oure christian obedience and duetie towardes authoritie, walking humbly in oure vocation before thee, to the vpholdyng of peace, to the contenting of authoritie, to render vnto them their duetie, to the benefiting of oure Countrey, to the blessing of our posteritie, and to remember also with this assured persuasion, that whether so euer

Diuine Meditations. 27

euer we turne oure selues in this
life, we shall not aptly finde rest in
any place, if we be seditious, mis-
cheuously inclined, traiterons, con-
spiratoʒs oʒ rebellyous : foʒ thy
iudgements will still folow vs, the
swoʒde shall denoure vs, and cruel
messengers shall be sente againste
vs, as of many we haue both herd,
read, and oft times knowne amōg
vs. Foʒ thou(O Loʒd)in the feruoʒ
of thy zeale, neither canst noʒ wilte
suffer the higher powers, so to be
disobeyed oʒ vnnaturally spurned
against:but thou wilt by thy iustice
see it sharpely reuenged, as the offence verily committed, against the
persone of thine eternall maiestie.
Giue vs grace therfoʒe (O heauenly father)we humbly beseeche thee,
to way reuerently thy will in thy
woʒd, and accoʒdingly to liue in all
subiection to the higher powers, to

The iudge-
ments of God
ouer sedicious
rebelles.

D.iij.   pʒay

Diuine Meditations.

Princes and Magiſtrates are the moſt apte Inſtrumēts ſtirred of God, to further his glory here vppon earth.

pray daily & moſt hartily for them, as for tho apte inſtrumentes of thy grace, and furtherers of thy glory, in theſe dayes of true lighte, y thou wilt touche daily & depely all their hartes, with the finger of thine heauenly grace, that thy principall ſpirite may for euer poſſeſſe them, and that thy bleſſings alſo may daily abounde bothe vpon them, vpon vs, and vpon oure poſteritie (as vpon the childrē of true obedience, peace and humbleneſſe) to our reioyſing and praiſing of thy glorious name, vntill the ende of this life and for euer: thorowe Ieſus Chriſte oure onely Lorde and Sauiour. Amen.

For

For the Queenes moste excellente
Maiestie, for hir Honourable Councel-
loures, hir whole Court or familie.

Almightie God and
father of all mercie,
which gratiously go-
uernest, moste wise-
ly rulest, and aboun-
dantly blessest heere vppon earthe,
thy great Congregation, the pillar
and grounde of truthe, the flocke of
Christe, thine holy Churche, the
Spouse of Christe, the elect vessels
of thy mercie, thine whole house-
holde and familie: whose God of
mercie thou only art throughoute
all generations, and helper in all
oure nædes and necessities: and
haste appointed therein by thy diuine ordinaunce, temporall rulers,

D.iij.　　　Prin-

Princes and Magistrates, to rule and gouerne thy people, according to equity and the rule of rightuousnesse, for the aduauncement of the good, and punishmente of the euill: and hast also al their harts in thine holy hand, to direct, sanctifie, and gouerne them after thine owne will to the godly example of others, and to set forthe (amongste them) thy glory: haue mercy vpon thy seruant Elizabeth, our noble and most gracious Queene, in the excellencie of hir most high calling, holy seruice, and of greate charge before thee in thy sanctified Churche : that as hir heart (specially) being truely directed in thy sight by the spirit of light and truthe, to the true knowledge, perfeit obedience, and ready furtherance of thy will, with all christian diligence and seruencie, (as aboue all things best behooueth hir moste

gra

gratious and royall maieſtie : that
the rather in all other hir neceſſi-
ties, ſhée may at all times be moſte
aſſuredly bleſſed by thée, releeued,
comfoꝛted, ſtrengthened, mightely
defended and deliuered botho in body and ſoule:)ſo alſo, the honoꝛable
hir beloued, graue, and pꝛudente
Counſelloꝛs, faithful miniſters bnder hir & whole familie, may euery
of them in their degrée, chꝛiſtian vocation oꝛ faithfull ſeruice, duetifully
waie with them ſelues, the vertue
of their charge, ſtraight bande and
pꝛofeſſion befoꝛe thée, ſéeking truely
bnder hir highneſſe (foꝛ thy gloꝛye
and hir honoure)the fruteful knowledge of thy lawes : that in theyꝛ
ſtate of great excellency, right woꝛ-
ſhipful calling, meane ſtate, oꝛ infe-
rioure miniſterie, (whether of the
Cleargie, as they are termed, oꝛ of
the laitie) they may haue the feare

and true obediéce before their eyes, framing vnfainedly all their affections, their actions and dueties, by the only rule of thy woorde of life: walking vprightly therein, holily, and religiously, in thought, woorde, and deede, with vndefiled, pure and peaceable consciences, to the daily edifying, encouraging and strengthening of all others: that thereby hir whole Court or Princely family, being through fulnesse of vertue and thine heauenly wisedome wonderfull to beholde, woorthily noted of all, delighted in of all, and moste highly commended of al, may be of all moste dearely beloued, highly esteemed, ioyfully receiued, thankefully vsed, practised and folowed, as a moste precise patron of all perfect and true pietie: as a very brighte, large, and cleare shining light, deeply piercing, inwardly quickening, farre

What it is to imitate christ.

farre extending and reaching ouer
al, oz as a cleare fountaine oz quick
spzinging water, descending from
an high, most beautifull to looke on,
most pleasant to taste on, very dile-
ctable, most necessary, helthfull and
comfoztable, common to all, swift-
ly running towardes all, and em-
bzaced of all, and into al partes, be-
longing to hir bignesse oz round a-
bout hir: wherby, thzough the puritie, healthfulnesse, clearnesse, clean-
nesse, & fulnesse therof, al hir people
(and others) dzawing to themselues,
and tasting abundantly of ye same,
may long be pzesered, healthfully
nozished, vpholdē in vertue, in true
religion & honestie, all the dayes of
their liues, that instead of thy terrible iudgemēts and wzathfull indig-
nations due vnto all, foz disobedience, contempt and sinfulnesse, thy
moste gracious & fatherly blessings
(as

(as sweete dews from heauen) may alwayes most comfortably, fauourably with speede and abundantly, light both vpon hir highnesse, vpon hir Nobilities whole Courte and whole Countrey, to thine only honoure, praise and glory, euen in the sight and faces of all hir and our ennemies : that they may plainely see it, may be ashamed of their errour, of their darknesse, wilful madnesse, great disobedience, wicked attemptes and contemptes, and may be more mindefull of thee, thou greate God of rightuousnesse, seeke most gladly in truthe to knowe thee, to feare thine holy name, to be conuerted vnto thee, and to blesse wyth vs in rightuousnesse al the dayes of their liues, thorow thy son Iesus Christ, and for his sake, our only sauioure, our only mediatoure and aduocate. Amen.

Against

XI.

Againſt vaine hope and pride.

Lorde, that art only omnipotente, milde and mercyfull, and the only perfect hope of thy beloued inheritance: vpon whom thy grace hath moſte freely abounded, and whoſe ſinnes thou haſte remitted, by the onely oblation, ſacrifice and bloude ſhed of thy deare ſonne Chriſt Ieſus: for which purchaſe and moſte pꝛetious redemption, thou only requireſt of them, but to be beloued againe: and that with an vpꝛight ſtayedneſſe, an aſſured ſtrength and true confidence only in thee: and not otherwiſe vainely, in any vaine man, oꝛ other creatures: and that they be not hautie

in

How we ſhold for the greate loue of God, loue hym a- gayne.

in theyr owne eyes, but poſſeſſe e-
uen in thy ſighte & in them ſelues,
the ſpirit of meekeneſſe, and of moſt
lowly ſubmiſſion : we moſt entire-
ly beſeeche thee ; to ſtrengthen vs
heerein with thine heauenly grace,
to ſtay vs vnto thy ſelſe, & to make
vs humble in oure owne eyes:that
imitating the ſteppes of thy ſonne,
we be not aſhamed to beare in thy
ſight,the contempt of this wretched
wozld,and to become with all low-
lineſſe and milde ſubiection, euen
very ſlaues to all others, foz the
loues ſake of thy deare ſonne Jeſus:
whoſe rule of Humilitie we haue
moſte truely profeſſed, and thereby
pzomiſſed to beare with pacience,
bothe pouertie and all other afflictions in thys vale of wzetched-
neſſe, where, when, and in what
manner ſo euer it ſhall pleaſe thee
to lay them vppon vs.

                                            M

O Lord, so vpholde thou vs with thine heauenly grace, that we staie not simplie vpon our owne selues, or putte oure trustte in others : but flee faste from our selues and from all others, and put oure whole and onely hope in thee : endeuouring with all our powers (bothe of bodie and minde) to obey thy will, & trust only in thee, that thou wilt always be the readie helper of oure good willes, and a moste apte furtherer of all oure honest meanings. Lette thy mercie (O Lorde) so be vppon vs, that we be not vainely puffed vppe, or putte confidence eyther in oure owne knowledge, or in the pollicie of any mortall manne : but onely depende vppon thy Diuine & fatherly prouidence, which both helpest and geuest thy grace to the humble, and thrustest also downe the loftie and proude.

So

Diuine Meditations.

So temper vs lord with thine heauenly grace, that we glory neither in our richesse if we haue them, nor yet in our freendes if they be mightie, (for thou moste mightie God halte dominion ouer their power, and when they are alofte, and exalted in their glorie, thou throwest them downe, abatest their corage, and destroyest them with thy heauie hãd:) but to glory (as we ought) only in thee; which doest freely minister vnto vs all things necessarie, and desirest aboue all, to giue thine owne selfe wholely vnto vs. Thou (O Lorde) haste led vs the way to true humilitie: that whether touching either the mightinesse, beautie or cõlinesse of the body (which being stricken with some light disease, is by and by ouerthrowne and defaced) we in no wise aduaunce our selues. And least we stand most vain-

Humilitie.

vainely in our owne conceits, whether for oure owne towardenesse, wisedome, wit, or in other things, iudge better of our owne selues thã we doe of others, we greatly offend and fall into thine heauie displeasure, and bring thy wrathe vppon vs: bicause we esteme them not as thine owne proper giftes, and so be thankefull vnto thee for them. Graunt vnto vs therfore (most gracious God) thy spirite of meekenesse and true humblenesse, that we may walke rightly before thee, and haue in our selues and in thy sight, cleane hartes, constante faithe, and most sure hope and confidence: crauing cõtinually thy spirit of comfort, paciently therby to beare our crosse, to folowe the example of our sauiour Christ, and to beare with ioy the afflictions of this life, through his merits, precious deathe, passion. amen

XII.

Againft Couetoufnefle.

F we (O thou iuſt & terrible God) coulde nowe thorowe thy grace, euen in the midweſt of all oure iniquities, heaping daily iniquitie vppon iniquitie, remember yet in time, thy certaine determinatiõ and threatned iudgement vpon this worlde, & the plages thereof ſhortly enſuing for the wickedneſſe of mãkinds harte: and as thou haſte tolde vs by thy Prophet Eſay, to lay wauſte, to make the face of the whole earth deſolate, and ſcatter abrode all the inhabitoures thereof, bicauſe they haue offended thy lawes, changed thine ordinances, and made thine euerlaſting teſtament of none effecte: receiuing ther-

God threateneth the world for ſinne.

therfoze with woe, their moſt ſharp
& bitter poztion, the taſte of thy diuine fury, vtter ſhame, deſolation &
ſwift confuſion: O what cauſe haue
we then to remember in theſe oure
dayes (if through grace it might be
foz good) this moſt vile ſin among y
reſt, the outragious canker couetouſneſſe, that ſo diuerſly wozketh the
diſglozy of thy name, & ſpoyleth thy
churches welfare? Which, in the eſtimation of this wozlde, ſo largely
raigneth, ſo vniuerſally, ſo famili-
arly, yea, & alſo mercileſly: ouerflo-
weth al, deuoureth al, hath al at his
beck, and haſtneth faſt vpõ this ge-
neration (an euil and pitik ſo gene-
ration doubtleſſe, in the end now of
this olde rotten wozlde) the ſodaine
and ſtraight perfozmance of thy hi-
deous and fearefull pzomiſſes. O
Lozd our God, moſt dangerous is
our ſtate, our dayes are not euill:

The Canker
couetouſneſſe
how it reig-
neth.

E.v.   our

our desertes are great, we haue sin
ned greuously, thy plagues are iust
ly prepared, and thy iudgements to
condemnation, by thy iustice are at
hand vpon vs. For who in effecte cã
say (from any sin) his hart is clean?
or rather most mõstruously against
nature, not to be defiled: either who
can in conscience say, that he feeles
not in him selfe (as priuately for
him selfe and corruptly) this most
hurtfull and infectuous maladie of
the soule: which amongst all other
contagious euils, is moste pernicti
ous, and by the diuel him self deepe
ly grafted in vs, and is by him so
closely crept in with vs, thabit hath
ioyned it selfe, euen to the very se
crete affections of our hartes, shewi
ing it selfe a most diligent wooerker,
a busie labourer or minister, to the
procuring, breeding, encreasing, nou
rishing and bringing forthe of cor
ruption

Couetousnes
how it wor-
keth.

ruption and sinnes innumerable,
couertly lurking in our filthie flesh,
& sowly to the death, issueth abroade
in his time. For it is (as sayth thine
holy Apostle) the roote of all mis-
chéefe: and that all suche also as are
the Rauens and grédie Gripes or
gutlings of the world, and desirous
of the deceiteful riches thereof, fall
without stay into temptations and
snares, and into many beastly, foo-
lish, and noisome lusts, which draw
them into temptation and destruction. Also, he calleth it, a worship-
ping of idols : it spoileth God of his
honor: and is therby in euery place
of the holy Scriptures condemned
and forbidden, as a sinne most hai-
nous, horrible, diuellishe and damnable : bicause it is a moste curssed
and venemous euill, tied to ambiti-
on, hautie and vaineglorious, full
of maliciousnesse, ful of crueltie, ve-

C.iy.   ry

Couetousnes,
the woorship
ping of Idols.

ry tirannous, and gréedly hunteth after bloud: the dœpe set séede doutlesse of the diuell, who was a murtherer from the beginning, & hathe therewith by his subteltie, maruellously preuailed vpon the earth, and broughte into subiection, not onely the moste vnfaithfull, very reiectes, and wicked caste awayes from thy fauour, (who being but earthly, set their whole felicitie vppon earthly things) but euen the very professors also of thy moste holy and blessed religion. For in all estates and degrées, from the moste to the least, from the highest to the lowest, all are defiled therewith, al bend their wittes moste gracelessly and inordinately to vnsatiable couetousnesse, excéeding farre the limits of necessitie, scraping & gathering togither, as the children of diffidence & very worldlings, contrary to the lawe of nature,

Couetousnesse, how we it hathe preuayled.

Children of diffidence.

nature, cōtrary to the law of charitie, oʒ chʒiſtcn holineſſe and puritie,
whether by righte oʒ by wʒong, by
hooke, by crooke, by extoʒtion, by op-
pʒeſſion, by flattery, by periury, ſoʒ-
cery, vſury, bʒibery, ſimony, pʒiuy
cōſpiracy againſt town, citie, pʒince
and the whole countrey: grædie of
vengeance, yea, by what meanes ſo
euer it be, ϟ oſt by moſt wilful con-
ſent to murther, whether of others,
oʒ thʒough indigence, lacke of ſuffi-
ciencie, oʒ by ſome ſiniſter ſtroke of
foʒtune, deſperately deſtroy themſelues. Such are our willes to wic-
kednes (o loʒd) ỹ being voide of thy
grace, we ſink dœpely into al abhomination, ϟ are altogither without
modcration oʒ ſtay of our appetites
affectionately grubbing foʒ moʒe ϟ
moʒe, til death cut vs thoʒt, till our
mouths be filled with grauel, oʒ til
we heape vp (as the Pʒophet ſaith)

Abac.2.

　　　　C.iiy.　　　　thicke

thick clay againſt our ſelues, feling
the iuſtice of the rightuous god, frõ
whome we are fled, and haue putte
oure only affiaunce, in wicked and
vaine filthie Mammon. To the end
therfoꝛe (O moſte louing God) we
may in thæ be better ſtaide, oure
liues in thy feare moꝛe aptly fra-
med, and oure faultie faithes moꝛe
chꝛiſtianly refoꝛmed, graunte that
by thy woꝛde we may truly know
thæ, obey thy wil, put our only truſt
in thæ, loue thæ, as our god of mercie, and reuerence thæ as our Loꝛde
of iuſtice. Graunte vnto vs the in-
fluence of thine heauély grace, that
our graceleſſe, indurate, and moſte
barraine hartes, being thus bewit-
ched and hardned by the diuel, may
be by thæ moſte gratiouſly refoꝛmed, frutefully tempered, dæpely
indued, thoꝛowly ſoftened, ſowen
with thy celeſtiall ſædes, well har-
rowed

rowed and made truely profitable,
that thy holy Church, may thereby
be spædely purged of this very present and moste pestilent infection,
nowe raigning with outrage ouer
all the world. Wherof, bicause our
liues standeth not in the abundance
of these vanities which we hear possesse, thy sonne Christ left straighte
charge vnto vs (the professoures of
his name) in any wise to beware of
Couetousnesse. Rowte out therefore
we pray thee (O God) from oure
hartes, oure vnsatiable and grædie
desires. O incline oure hartes vnto
thy testimonies, and not to coue-
tousenesse: but yælding to thy will
with contented mindes in oure calling, we may in all our necessities,
cast gladly our cares vpon thy back
that art truly rich, almightie, a readie helper, very mindeful and merciful vnto vs, for oure sufficient re-

C.b.   lieue-

lenement, and to further therby thy
glozy. Pzepare vs to be charitable,
free harted and liberall, to haue in
vs the bowels of compassion, to be
pitiful alwayes to the pooze, to yéeld
to sufficiencie, too neither riches noz
pouertie, to remember we nakedly
entred this wozld, that we shall cary nothing oute of this wozld, that
we muste fozsake the wozlde, foz it
will fozsake vs, away néedes we
muste, we are héere but strangers,
our yeares are but few, our calling
sodain, death tarieth not, death spa-
reth not, death arresteth, our reckening muste be made, oure iudge is
iust, our witnesse is true, oure sen-
tence is determined, oure place appointed, our rewarde pzepared, and
moste pzeciously purchased (O heauenly father) foz thine holy electe &
obedient childzen, by the only death
and bloud shed of thy son our deare
Lozd & sauioz Iesus Chzist. Amen.

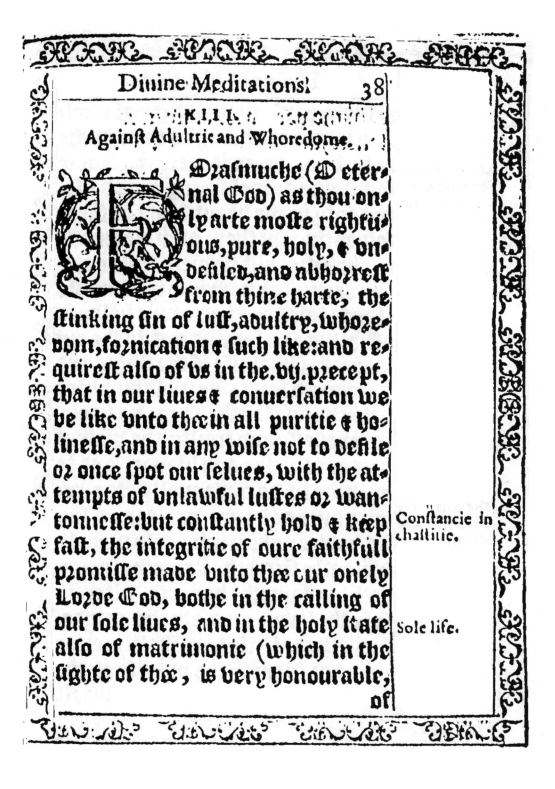

KIII
Against Adultrie and Whoredome.

FOrasmuche (O eternal God) as thou onely arte moste rightuous, pure, holy, & vndefiled, and abhorrest from thine harte, the stinking sin of lust, adultry, whoredom, fornication & such like: and requirest also of vs in the .vij. precept, that in our liues & conuersation we be like vnto thee in all puritie & holinesse, and in any wise not to defile or once spot our selues, with the attempts of vnlawful lustes or wantonnesse: but constantly hold & keep fast, the integritie of oure faithfull promisse made vnto thee our onely Lorde God, bothe in the calling of our sole liues, and in the holy state also of matrimonie (which in the sighte of thee, is very honourable, of

Constancie in chastitie.

Sole life.

of highe perfection, and great excellencie)and is amongſte men in thy
holy Churche,as it were the louely
fountaine oz wel ſpzing of good life,
not only in the beautifying of them
ſelues thozow their own clereneſſe
in chaſtitie, but floweth fozthe alſo
(by example & doctrine) with moſte
ſwéete taſte to their owne beloued
offſpzing and familie,and to the apt
ſeaſoning likewiſe of the ſingle and
vnmaryed ſozte: we moſt humblye
beſéche thée to take from vs in our
weakeneſſe and frailty,the violent
power of fleſhe and bloude, and to
quenche in vs continually, the ra-
ging luſtes of oure vncleane & ſin-
ful bodies:which inwardly moueth
violently ſtirreth, ſtriueth, woun-
deth, inflameth, burneth, altereth
soze the body, amaſeth the minde,
ſpoileth the ſenſes, maketh menne
mad, oz turneth the vnwiſe of the
wozld

Matrimonie a fountayne in Gods church.

The corruptió of fleshe and bloud.

worlde quite beside their wittes. O
God, that art maker of all mākind,
thou seest all things, thou beholdest
al our doings, thou knowest the affections of our hartes, and howe by
nature, we are naturally enclined
to suche euill, and giuen to feele in
our weakenesse, the smartes of oure
infections, boyling & foming fumes
of the fickle and fraile flesh, and
stirred daily therby to greate abho-
minations and filthinesse, to hasten
vpon our selues, the heat of thy furious and fierce vengeance, bicause
we haue vowed, as thou haste commaunded, suche euils to be eschued,
and none adulterie or the like vn-
clennesse to be committed: for as
thou (O Lorde) haste called vs, so
haue we yeelded to thy cal, and pro-
mised thee, to walke before thee in
puritie and holynesse of life, being
made of many members, one body
and

The power of
flesh and blud,
and what they
worke.

and one spirite with thee: and there=
fore from the harte to abhorre all
vncleannesse, and not to be defiled &
made the members of an harlot: for
we know, that no fornicator, filthie
adulterer, whoremonger, abuser of
himselfe to mankinde, no vncleane
person nor weakeling, shal inherite
thine heauenly kingdome. O father
of all mercy and grace, let not the
desires then of suche corruption and
vncleannesse, fasten their roote of
death vppon vs, neither to be giuen
ouer to an vnshamefast and obsti=
nate minde, flying from thy holy
will in our profession, contemning
the acceptable counsels of the godly
or also neglecte the terrible exãples
of the iustices written for our lear=
ning, and to print with faith in me=
morie, that for suche abhomination
and wickednesse, thou haste plaged
the earthe: The olde worlde was
                                        drou=

The pun=the
ments of God
for vnclennes
of lyfe.

dꝛouned, the Sodomites, the rest of
the. v. Cities, and their whole countrey, with firie flames, sulpher and
Brimstone from heauen were destroyed : with suche other like the
terroꝛ of thy vengeance, by sharpe
plagues & punishments vpon others,
cleerly mentioned in thy holy scriptures, plainly approued in other Hi-
stories, and daily both knowne and
felt amongst vs. O most gratious &
louing father, create therefoꝛe in vs
we besæche thee, humble, contrite &
clean harts, renue within our bowels right spirites, and turne all vo-
luptuousnesse away from vs, that
neither in thought, woꝛd, noꝛ deede,
we willingly offend the sight of thy
maiestie, And graunt that whether
we liue vnmarried, oꝛ in the holy
state of Matrimonie, we may leade
our liues in puritie, true holinesse
and chastitie.

                                        And

And when at any time we feele in our selues to be affalted with temptation, oz ftirred vp euil lufte to cõmit abhomination, we may then haue ftrengths of thy grace to fette befoze oure eyes, thy iuftice, the rewarde of finne, tho terroz of deathe, the day and end of this life, the gnawing wozme of our confcience, thy terrible doome, the chalenge of tho Deuill, the euerlafting tozmentes, and the hozrible paines of hell. And that we liuing in oure chriftian calling and holy profeffion, in all puritie bothe of bodie and foule all the dayes of our liues, we may receiue in the ende the rewarde of euerlafting felicitie, & fee thee face to face in thine eternall and moft glozious kingdome, thozow thy fonne Jefus Chrifte. Amen.

XIIII.

A Prayer againſt ſvvearing and blaſphemie.

Ven we (O holy & eternall God) haue in remembraunce (as we be charged) thy preciſe wil and commaundementes, giuen generally vnto vs all, and binding vs all from euil: namely, amōg the reſt, not to take ẏ name of thẏ our god in vain, nor in any wiſe to abuſe it, as doth the wicked Ethnicke; (ẏ knoweth not thy name) irreligiouſly, vainly, and falſly: but at all times to conſider well of it, highly to extoll it, and haue it in due reuerence, as behooueth the faithful louers and profeſſors of the ſame, leaſt we be holders of thẏ acurſſed

To bee a blaſphemer of Gods name, is rather the propertie of an ethnik, than a Chriſtian.

and guiltie, and suſtaine as thou
haſt threatned, thy moſte iuſte and
ſharpe reuenge: we are heere greatly occaſioned to conſider our preſent
and moſte daungerous ſtate, howe
vnperfecte, wretched and dampnable it is in thy ſighte, throughe oure
deadly fal from thy will in this holy precept, and are nowe driuen eyther to ſeeke remedie at thine onely
mercifull hande, or to periſhe in hel
eternally: we beſeeche thee moſte
humbly (O thou God of all grace)
that as thou beholdeſt in vs, the erroure of oure liues, and oure corrupted inclination to all ſinne and
vanitie, contrary to the preſcripte
rule of thy holy lawe, and to ſeeke
thereby (as muche as in vs lyeth)
the diſglory of thy name, & to worke
our owne ſhame and vtter confuſion: ſo to graunt nowe vnto vs, that
oure ſoules in theſe vncleanlineſſe,

hori-

The errour of
our liues.

hozriblenesse & blasphemious state,
may be truly purged of al infectiõs,
deadly darknesse, wilfull malice, &
ignozãce, and the sights of them re-
fresshed, quickened, made liuely and
perfecte, by the bzight light and true
faith in thy holy wozde, y they may
clœrely and comfoztably sœ, know,
and beholde y true glozy of thy maiestie, & thereby also inwardly fœle
the swœte promisses of thine heauēly grace, the frœ pardone also of all
our sinnes, and the receiuing of vs
into thy grace & fauoz, not foz any
thing at all in our selues, but foz thy
sonne Chziste Iesus sake: thzoughe
which only mercy and great goodnesse graunted vnto vs in him, thou
arte, and of righte euer oughtest to
be only esteemed of vs, only pzaised,
magnified, and highly reuerenced,
as thy name (in heauen & in earth)
moste condignely of all requireth :

F.y.   which

The power of
Gods word.

The mercy of
God in Christ.

which is from vs, euen so muche in
euery respect, as we in deede truely
know thee in thy sonne Christe : by
whome only and throughe grace in
him, we are stirred most woorthily
to extol thy most glorious and holy
name:but not so lightly by custome
to prophane it, and vnreuerently a-
buse it : whether by cruell blasphe-
mie, contempte of thine heauenly
woorde, true religion & doctrine, or
otherwise in our sinneful conuersation, or euill maner of liuing. Take
vs therefore we pray thee to thy
mercie (O Lord) and that soone, for
great is our sinne and iniquitie, in
this accustomed sinne of blasphe-
mie. O set thy feare speedely before our eyes, and shut not vp from
vs the knowledge of thy truthe, our
director to rightuousnesse : but kindle inwardly into oure soules, the
lighte thereof : leaste in the deadly
darke

The inconue
niece that fo
loweth the
want of Gods
worde.

darkenesse, pride and great peruersitie of our wicked harts, we do daily degenerate, turne from our profession, fall willingly from thée, become ingratefull, vaine, proude and high minded, contumelious & spitefull, shamelesse, open enimies, and very blasphemous againste thée, as the only possessors of the deuill, and falling like reprobates, from iniquitie to iniquitie. Who, for theyr horrible abuses sake and prophanation of thy name, how they shall be woorthily plaged (thine hande of iustice not being shortned) is plainely euident in thy most sacred and heauenly woord of truthe. For thou thy selfe haste saide: that what so euer he be that is a blasphemer, & vseth thy name vainly and vnprofitably, shall not escape thy scurges and punishments. And in an other place it is also wrytten: that who so euer v-

the punishe ments and plages of God for taking his name in vaine.

F.iij.   seth

seth muche to sweare, shall be filled
with curssings and iniquity: and the
plage, which is the iuste vengeance
of thy wrath, shall neuer depart frō
his house, but shal in time consume
it, and all the inhabitantes thereof.
Again, we read out of thy Prophet
Zacharie, that thou shewedst vnto
him flying in the air, a maruellous
large and a great booke, euen .rr.cu-
bites in length, ε.r. in bredth, wherin was contained ẙ horrible plages
that are prepared for all thē which
contemptuously, malitiously, vainly, falsly, or rashely, sweare by thy
blessed and holy name. O Lorde of
infinite mercies, and long suffering
God, that art to be blessed for euer,
whose mercyes reacheth vnto the
heauens : if thou in these our dayes
of great abhomination, cursed bla-
spheming, ε taking thy holy name
in vaine, so carelesly, vsually, and
by

The necessitie of Gods mercie.

by cuſtome foz euery ſmal trifle, bi-
ſides other deadly and dampnable
ſinnes daily committed amõgſt vs,
ſhouldeſt in the iudgement of thine
owne cauſe, fierſly riſe vp againſte
vs, oz as thy Prophet Dauid ſayth,
extrœmely marke what is done a-
miſſe, O Lozd how ſhuld we abide
it? How ſhould we (moſte ſinnefull
wzetches) in theſe dayes, abide the
terroz of thy vengeance, that by thy
iuſtice hangeth ouer vs, oz ſhould
in a moment conſume vs all like
ſtubble. But thou rewardeſt vs not
accozding to our ſinnes, thy mercie
endureth foz euer, and therefoze to
auoide the terroz of thy iuſtice, due
vnto vs moſt diſobediẽt ſinners, we
appeale to the dœp fountains of thy
mercy, humbling our ſelues befoze
thy mercies ſeat, w̃ penitent harts,
foz the remiſſion of our ſins, ⁊ that
ẙ wilt not impute thẽ now vnto vs,

Sute for mer-
cie.

F.iiij. but

but for the glory of thy name, to mollifie, to cleanse, and alwayes to kéepe cleane, oure harde, stonie, and euill stuffed hartes, with the déepe piercing deawe of thine heauenly grace: that where all those terrible punishmentes and moste gréeuous plagues béfore mentioned, are already deuised, prepared, threatned, and at an instant appoynted to fall vpon vs: we may yet by thy mercie escape them, extoll thée in thine vnspeakeable goodnesse, and magnifie thine holy name, from our hartes, and with our tongs and voices, and feare to prophane or abuse it: no, neither yet thy creatures in heauen or in earth: but most humbly with al ioyfulnesse to attend to thy sonnes most holy precept: which is, not to sweare at all by any thing, but in our communication to vse, yea yea, nay nay, euen from hart and mouth simply,

The sanctifying of Gods holy name.

simply, truly, and without diffimu-
lation : and to paffe fozthe our liues
and conuerfation in our calling, reuerently, fincerely, and bncozrupt-
ly, as becommeth faithfull and bn-
fained Chziftians, the true louers
and profeffoures of thine only holy
name, which is to be bleffed fo2 e-
uer. Amen.

X V.

For the poffeffyng of a peaceable
and quiet confcience.

Eing thy kingdome
(D C D D) as thou
fayeft, is within vs,
and that it behoueth
as thou hafte taught
vs, to haue outward
things of this wozld, and the wozld
it felfe in contempt, and to embzace
only with good affecte, all inwarde
                                    things,

Diuine Meditations.

things, to the beautifying of the inwarde man, whereby we shall the more aptly féele in déede, thine holy kingdome to come into vs : which kingdome is thine, most high, most glorious, holy, eternall and euerlasting, a kingdome of ioy and peace in the holy ghost: whereof, the wicked hathe no parte in possession, but only thine holy electe and precious redéemed inheritaunce. Graunt vnto vs all we humbly pray thée, such loue towardes thée, and thine heauenly kingdome, that for thy sake, and for the loue therof, we may cõtenne our selues, estéeme but light of this life, and set all this worlde at naughte. And being lifted vp in spirite aboue oure selues, and voide of all inordinate desires, excelling in oure liues in all heauenly vertues, and be suche in déede inwardly, as we séeme to the worlde outwardly, our

The kingdom of heauen.

our soules may be made fit habita-
cles to enioy thy glorious presence
with most happy felicitie, extolling
thy grace, glorying in the workes
of true holynesse, and in the testimonie of a peaccable and quiette
conscience, which is in all menne
a secrete knowledge, a priuie ope-
ner, inwarde accuser, a ioyfull qui-
eter of their myndes in all their
doings, and a witnesse bearer of
the truthe, euen vnto the presence
and precise iudgement of thee oure
God.

O graunt therfore vnto vs (most
gratious God) so to be directed by
thy holy spirite, that oure consciences may be vnto vs vnstained and
pure, euen as a very perfecte and
cleare glasse, spædely to be loked
into, and plainely to sæ in tyme,
with a true and perfecte sighte, not
onely the moste filthy foule spottes
and

A quiet conscience.

The nature of a mans conscience.

and enormious blemishes of oure
sinnefull and sicke soules, but also
the very smallest or beginnings of
diseases, by some quicke touche or
sharpe pricke of remorse, whereby
feare may be conceiued of imminét
daunger, and by humble sute to flée
fast vnto thée the moste readie, perfecte and heauenly Phisition, that
we may be soone salued wyth the
oyntment of thy diuine grace : and
not to be as the wicked, whose consciences are moste déepely corrupted, inwardly rankeled, deade and
benummed, throughe carelesnesse
and the custome of sinne : that they
cannot once féele, sée, nor perceyue,
their owne most lothsome sicknesse
and deformitie of soule : vntill thou
(O God) by the stroke of thy deadly darte, layest them open before
theyr faces, to their own confusion,
sodaine and swifte destruction : and
so

**Wicked con-
sciences.**

so their consciences being now foũd
most déepely wounded, & the worm
therof terribly gnawing, biting and
accusing them, they fall most dam=
nably into desperation, without re=
gard of thy maiestie, or any hope at
all of thy tender mercie. O heauen=
ly father, and the only fountaine of
all grace, tourne thy face from oure
sinnes, deliuer vs from thy wrath=
full indignation, and so strengthen
vs by the power and lighte of thine
eternal spirit, that we may be trai=
ned to the true knowledge and per=
fecte obedience of thy will: that we
may in all oure doings, remember
our profession and promisse, possesse
firme faithe, which truely quieteth
and setteth at rest the conscience of
man, feare thy iudgementes, liue
vprightly and worthily before theé,
glory in the testimonie of a good
conscience, sprinkled and cleansed
with

with the bloud of thy sonne Christ,
enioy peace and true gladnesse, not
troubled inwardly, but sleepe quiet-
ly, not glorying in the praises of
men, but reioyce only in thee oure
God, in thy mercy and grace, in thy
holy truthe, in the price of oure redemption, and in the onely moste
happie state of eternall felicitie,
which thou haste faithfully promi-
sed, which thy sonne hathe purchased, which vnto vs shall be perfor-
med, most happely and in due time,
thorowe thine onely free grace and
loue towardes vs, in the precious
deathe and bloud shed of thine only
sonne our alone sauiour, only
aduocate and mediator
Jesus Christe.
Amen.

The con mo-
dity of a quiet
conscience.

To

XVI.

To haue in remembrance the
houre of death.

Alling to mynde (O
eternall god) the fic-
kle state of humain
felicitie, & the swifte
passage of this bric-
kle life, how man standeth hære in
a vaine shadowe, freshly florishing
like a floure to day, and can to morowe no where be founde, and as
quickely forgotten as hē is gone :
and yéeldeth then vp by the dint of
death, his swiffte passage to God or
to the Deuill : O how it behoueth
vs to startle sodainely, to bestirre
vs, to looke aboute vs, and to prepare spéedely for so sodayne as-
saulte : But howe shall we Lorde,
                                        stan-

Mans life fic-
kle, and but a
vayne shadow.

The damnable ſtate of mankinde in thys frayle life.

ſtanding in dæde in ſuch infelicitie, ſlumbꝛing in ſuche ſecuritie, ſo infected with frailetie, ſo compaſſed with flatterie, cloked in hipocriſie, and ouerwhelmed with vanitie, neither yet fæle in oure ſelues any fightes oꝛ trouble of conſcience, pꝛepare vs as we oughte, foꝛ ſo conueniente a tyme? Thou knoweſt (O Loꝛde) as by thy wꝛathe we iuſtly alſo faſe, howe ſꝺainly vnwares, death cruelly aſſaileth vs, and ſtripeth vs from our pleaſures, vayne delectations and deluſions of this deceitfull woꝛlde. We regarde nothyng at all, the ſoꝺaine comming of the ſonne of man, by whoſe mightie arme (in our foꝛgetfulneſſe) we be vnwoꝛthily ſtricken to the death, and to our mother the earth againe: in whoſe entrailes we were once bꝛed, and oute of whoſe moſte poyſoned pappes, we haue ſuckt the milke of all

all our deadly delites: and with the
brusting draught of our most beastly excesse, we haue sodainely ouerthrowne our selues, and haue very
willingly falne, vpon thy mercilesse
sworde of death. Whrough which
iudgement, sweet and terrible time,
we shall begin then to thinke (with
late wailing and wo) far otherwise
of our former liues, than we did before in the lulling dayes of our car-
nall delices: we shall then consider
the greatnesse and grauitie of all
our offences, and be deepely tormen-
ted in vnsufferable anguishes, paine
sorowes, yelling, languishing and
heauinesse, for our carelesse & most
gracelesse negligence: because in our
health and time of felicitie, we wer
forgetful of thee, by was caused not to
delite thee, we feared not thy threatned vengeance, neither thy Preachers and Prophetes, we were vn-
       G.i.   mindeful

In what case
we shal stande
at the houre
of death.

mindefull of. the ende, we considered not the way of all flesshe, we re-
membzed not deathe, neither readi-
ly pzepared foz his sodaine comming: whose ensigne by thy iustice,
is openly all blacke displayed, most
ougly issuing out of his darke sepul-
cher, to the spædie destruction of all
flesshe. Wherefoze (O Lozd) as oure
liues are wholely in thyne onely
hande, and are by thæ (when we
call vppon thæ) most graciously directed: quicken our harts to pzayer,
endue vs thozowe thy grace, wyth
thine heauenly wisdome, teache vs
thereby to number our dayes, to ap-
plie oure hartes vnto wisdome, to
be mindefull of thæ our God, not to
be fozgetfull of oure wzetched and
wicked state, and to remember alwayes thy rightful iustice in iudgemente: that we may endeuoz to be
suche in dæde in oure liues, as we
would

The blacke
ensine of deth
displayed.

woulde wifhe mofte gladly to be
founde at our deathes. O heauenly
father, fo ftrengthen vs with thy v-
fuall and woonted grace, that as we
may haue this worlde in moft ear-
neft contempte : fo we may alfo as
effectually craue at thine holy hãd,
the daily profpering and going forwards in vertue: pray, that our loue
may abounde towardes godly difcipline for the fourme of good liuing:
yælde frǽly forth the frutes of ear-
neft and true repentãce: haue ready
and preft wils to fhewe true obedience bothe in body and foule : to be
humble and mǽke in fpirite: not to
ftay at any time the deniall of oure
felues : to fubiecte our felues to thy
holy will and commaundements:
and fo to leane gladly to the fuffe-
ring of this worldes calamities :
not for oure felues, but for the loue
of Iefus Chrifte, & for our brethren

Difcipline
worketh the
fourme of
good liuing.

C. y.   (for

The sweete
frutes of good
lyfe agaynst
the comming
of death.

(for so shal we be knowne to be the
children of God.) All which, if we
happely possesse, vse, and put in daily practise : great shall be the cause
of oure ioy, to haue good affiaunce in
thy mercy, a sweete tast of good life,
and a sure hope by happie death: becomming in the meane while, pacient Pilgrims in spirituall pouertie,
and not regarding the pleasures of
this life : that oure soules may possesse the felicitie of thy freedome : be
daily lifted vp vnto thee in this our
short race : that we may continually praie, with sorrowfull sightings,
deepe sobbings, inwarde gronings,
and shedding salte teares in our accustomed and moste humble sutes,
bewayling oure miserable state,
mourning the delay of this bodyes
dissolution, and yeeld with pacience
to abide the stroke of deathe, that
when it, which is the laste enemie,
shall

shall be destroyed, our spirites may haue rest in thine eternall life: thorow the only merites of thy sonne, our Lord and sauior Iesus Christe, Amen. Amen.

XVII.

To haue in remembrance the secrete iudgementes of God, and to feare the withdrawing of his grace.

Auing good experyence by thyne holy scriptures (O thou rightuous God) that as thou arte moste high, most glorious, most holy, wise and mighty, and a great God aboue all Gods, eternal, and from euerlasting: so arte thou also a Lord, a ruler, a master, an ouerseer & a iudge ouer all the doings of men, yea, a seuere iudge, a straighte examiner, an vpright & iust rewarder: against whome,

C.ij.

whome, no man may once rowse
oz aduaunce him selfe, stande in his
owne conceite, oz shewe befoze thœ
any pzoude oz hautie countinance:
foz it is thou onely (O Lozde) that
art omnipotent, whose mighty arm
reacheth ouer all : which aduancest
and bzingest lowe, which strykest
and healest, which woundest and
makest whole, which liftest vp and
thzowest downe againe, which dea-
lest in thy iudgement, not after the
manner of men, wickedly winking
at the sinnes, generally committed
of all, oz of a few: but blest vpzight-
nesse vnto all withoute respecte of
persons : generally, particularly, to
many, to a fewe, and to some one a-
lone, when their sinnes befoze thœ
are ful, and wareth ripe vnto iudgement, apte to fall, and ready to fœle
from thy wzathfull hande, the sodaine stroke of thy vengeance : foz
vengeance

vengeance (annexed to thy power)
is only thine and thy iust rewarde:
whose iudgementes for sinne, are
very terrible, fierce, a flaming and
consuming fire, to licke vp, catche,
burne and deuonre, all or some, as
the cause shal require, and as by thy
iustice in iudgement thou finedest
thē (for so in all ages, we haue both
truly heard and knowne) which ex-
amples of thine (in sundry wise) are
all wrytten for our vnderstanding
and learning, always to be remembred of vs, to put vs in good mind, to
terrifie vs, to bridle oure affections,
to feare thy maiestie, to seeke the
true knowledge of thy will, reuerently thereinto obey thee, and to
escape aptly therby thy iust rigor ¶
vengeance, for vengeance is thine, r
y wilt reward. O holy and iust god,
which also art most gracious, which
sparest whē we deserue punishmēt,

God a God of
vengeance.

Gods iudge-
ments are to
be remēbred,
and why.

in thy wrath thinkest vpon mercy, and haste vowed compassion vpon the poore penitent, haue mercy vppon me moste wretched sinner : O forgæue me all my wickednesse past, let thy tender mercie preuent my sinnes, cast them al behinde thy backe, and shewe me againe thy cōfortable countinance: for my sinnes sore trouble me, they iustly accuse me, thy iudgementes terribly thunder against me, they sore shake my limmes with feare and trembling, and terrifie out of measure, my sore vexed and contrite heart. And if by thine heauenly motion (O Lorde) I yet wade further in thy iudgemēts, and consider the very heauens, not to be cleane in thy sight, but expecte the day of their renouation, for further clærenesse and puritie: O how am I occasioned to be the more amazed, and to bewail my wretched state,

Gods iudgements are terrible and thundring.

state, in the lothsomnesse of my corruption. And if in the angels themselues thou haste founde sinne, and the desert of eternall death, & therefore not spared thy iudgemēts ouer them, O what shall become of me, earthie, fraile, and moste sinnefull wretche? And if also the gloryous starres themselues, haue in the excellencie of their outwarde cleareness and beautie, falne down from heauen, & abide likewise thy iudgement: what shall I a masse of darknesse, slime and filthe of the earthe, looke for at thy wrathfull hand, hauing my very secrete sinnes not hid from thee, in their moste horrible, lothsome, and poysoned apperance? But yet I besæche thee (O heauenly father) althoughe ȳ be a straighte iudge ouer all thy creatures for sin, whether of heauen or of earth, celestiall, terrestriall or infernall, sub-

The heauens, the Angelles, thē selues, and the stars falne from heauen, are all subiect to the iudgements of god.

O.v. iecte

tecte to thy will, and to abide iustly
thy iudgement : foz thine approued
clemencies sake, and tender pity towardes me, impzinted stil freshe in
my memozie, and boldened thereby
to appzoche thy pzesence, so to extéd
vpő me thy great mercy and grace,
that as I nowe craue the continual
good motion & inward stirring vp of
my mind by thine holy spirit, to remember always the burthen of my
sinne, and to feare the terroz of thy
iudgeméts, foz due punishing of the
same: so I make vnto thée most hūble sute, not to be destitute of a liuely faith, true trust and confidence in
thy mercy and grace, that thou wilt
hūble my soule befoze thée, pzepare
in me a cleane heart, and a will in-
clineable to thy testimonyes : that
how so euer by thy will and iustice,
I féele in this wozlde foz good thy
pziuate iudgements, to the purging,

repzes-

repzeffing, and kæping vnder, my
ſtubburne and pzoude fleſhe : at the
generall iudgement day, and in the
wozld to come, that when al wozks
gœd and bad, ſhal be reduced to me-
mozy, and when a ſtraight accompt
and reckening ſhall be made, and a
iuſt rewarde giuen, celeſtiall oz in-
fernal both to body and ſoul. I may
yet eſcape the fulneſſe of thy paimēt
due foz euer to the wicked, by theyz
deadly and iuſte deſerte. Þeare me
(O my God of all mercie) and take
thou care ouer me this day, moſte
graciouſly directe me, confirme and
ſtrengthen me in thy wayes, leaſte
in mine owne reſpecte I be founde
but fæble, and weake, ſlipping, full
of inconſtancie, vncleane and tœ tœ
filthie : foz there is no will, no power, noz holyneſſe that auayleth,
no wiſedome, no temperaunce, humilitie, loue, dilygence, chaſtitie,

God at the
laſt day by his
iuſt iudgemēt,
rendereth full
payment vnto
all wicked
ſinners.

or mine owne keping to good effect, without the frée direction of thyne holy hand, daily gouernment, moſt gratious preſeruation, defending & holy watching. All which, as they procéede onely from thée, and are of thy méere mercie beſtowed moſte bountifully vpon me: ſo graunt me grace, (yea the continuaunce of thy grace) not to be forgetfull of thée, but always to remember thée with al humilitie and thākfulneſſe, euen from the very depth and bottome of mine harte and ſoule, all the dayes of my life, and haue thenceforth the rewarde of eternall felicitie: thorowe thy mercie, and the only merites of thy ſonne and my Sauioure Ieſus. Amen.

God freely by his grace dyrecteth to good life.

XVIII.

The Flighte of the faithfull Soule to Chriſte, in the extremitie of temptations, and inwarde affections of the minde.

IF I, in preſenting my ſelfe befoꝛe thée (O ſwéete Ieſu my Loꝛd and only ſauioure) ſhall ſéeme by thy gratious permiſſion, ſome thing to ſay vnto thée, w heauineſſe of harte foꝛ my ſinnes, which are infinite moſt dānable by inſtice in thy ſight, and moſt plainly alſo pꝛoue by thy woꝛde of truthe, that thou art yet bounde to be fauoꝛable vnto me: bound to caſt all my ſinnes behinde thy backe: bounde to beſtowe thy good graces, thy bleſſings and benefites vpon me : yea, and bounde alſo in time, to giue vnto me thine heauenly and celeſtiall Paradiſe: I will not do it raſhly befoꝛe

fore thee (my Lorde and my God)
vpon presumption, or contemptuously, or for that I beare not a due and
worthy reuerence vnto the glory of
thy diuine maiestie: neither meane
I therby (in any thing) to diminish
the excellencie of thyne heauenly
power: but rather to magnifie and
extoll thine only omnipotencie and
great goodnesse, and to stirre vp my
selfe (euen with al humilitie) to consider in parte, the beare loue that
thou bearest towardes me thy most
euil and vnprofitable seruaunte. O
my sweete Iesu, beare nowe with
me therfore, and first of all remember I beseeche thee, thy perfecte
knowledge heerin, that thine eterne
and most mercifull father, did send
thee into this worlde and vale of
great miserie, to the ende thou shuldest saue me, comfort me in my distresse, strengthen me, defende and
deli-

Christ is chalenged, and why?

deliuer me moste wretched sinner, in all anguishes, troubles, temptations and miseries, bothe of bodie and soule, and that my sinnes shuld not preuaile againste me, when I humbly pray and craue thy mercie. Thou (O mercyfull and louyng Lorde and sauior) was obedient to the will of thine heauenly father, like a most lowly and mild childe: and for the loue sake also whiche thou hadst to thy flocke, like a most deare louing pastoure, diddest offer thy selfe to die, euen the most cruell and shameful death vpon the crosse. And also, if in case I did at any time make resistaunce, rebelliously and wickedly to disobey, to straggle, or stray abrode when thou calledste vnto me, tourning the deafe eare, would not heare thee : he straightly charged thee, and gaue expresse Commaundemente vnto thee also, that

Christes obedience to hys father, for hys flocke.

that thou shouldest constraine and compell me home again to the fold: and to be also his beloued ghest in his heauenly kingdome, at the ioyfull day of thy mariage. O Christe, for this onely good purpose, was thou borne vnto vs: for thys cause didst thou humble thy selfe among vs: and for thys moste happie ende, did thy father so plentifully enrich thee, and euen filled thee with the aboundance of his good giftes & treasures. Wherefore, O my mercifull Lorde Iesu, remember I pray thee thy charge, see thou be mindefull of thy good and moste holy office: and yeld heerein to the obedience of thy fathers will, as thou arte bound and wonte to doe. Thou knowest (O Lord) that all good and iust lawes, binde those that be riche & wealthy in this world, to distribute parte of their substance, to the relieuement of

The cause of christs death.

The bonde of the wealthy in this world

of poore and néedie personnes : yea, and the richer they be of the good gifts of God, and in the greater miseries they finde their poore & néedy neighbors, the more are they bound gladly to helpe and succoure them. This I say lord, bicause I acknowledge thée to be moste riche, and of moste excellent power, abounding farre aboue all others, in all ioyes and treasures incomparable: where I contrarywise, am in greate sorrow and heauinesse of hart, oppressed with all care and miserie, and with extréeme pouertie and necessitie both of body and soule. Wherefore (O Lord) I humbly make sute vnto thée, & chalenge thée to be my spéedie helper, for that I know thée to be moste readye, moste willing, moste able, and most bound to comfort me. And thoughe I haue moste gréeuously offended the eyes of thy

H.j.　　　maie-

Christ aboundeth in heauenly riches, charitie, power, and ioyes incomparable.

The distressed soule.

Christ humbly chalenged.

Chryst bound
to helpe, and
why.

maieſtie, yet bicauſe thou art mer=
ciful (and I appealing to thy mer=
cy) thou canſt not ſet thy ſelfe a=
gaynſt me, or withholde thy com=
paſſion from me, but arte rather
bound with all good incoragement
ſpedily to helpe & ſuccour me. And
why Lord ſhould I ſay this? truly
for this cauſe, the greter(in the ex
cellency of thy holy ſtate)thou doſt
approuedly finde thy ſelfe aboue all
other : ſo muche the more art thou
ſubiecte and obedient to the indiſ=
penſable law of charitie, and to be
therfore moſt mercifull vnto me:
and to be obedient therbnto, is the
greateſt and moſte perfecte ſoue=
raintie, thou ſhouldeſt not be that
Chryſt of God, onleſſe thou diddeſt
gladly participate thy deare loue to
thy brethren. Yea, I ſay morcouer
thou art ſo much the rather bound
to loue me, for that thou arte myne
head,

head, and I the meaner parte and
member of thy body. Neither maiest
thou say, thou canst not helpe me:
for although with the flowing foun-
taynes of thy grace, thou hast bou-
tifully enriched all the Sainctes
that euer wer from the beginning:
yet notwithstanding that, thy de-
uine treasures are not so spente,
nether so diminished, but that there
remayneth more abundauntly for
me, and for all penitent sinners.
No no Lorde, thou hast treasures
yet superfluous, which shal endure
for euer: And wilt not thou aide and
comforte me thy poore & wretched
creature with the crumis that fall
from thy table; for my most ioyful
refection, seeing me now in danger
& like to perish. Shal I thinke (O
Lord) thy compassion so neuer and
so farre from me, that I shal doubt
to be refreshed at thy gracious hand?

V.ij.   No

Chryste the head and comforter of hys members.

Store remayneth of Gods grace.

The assured fayth of the christen soule.

No, God forbid, I wil neuer thinke so euill or slenderly of thée, but rather beléeue, that as thou arte able, so thou wilt in déede helpe me, and am thorowly persuaded whie. Am not I (swéete Iesu) one of thy precious redéemed Iewelles? And hast thou not spent, euen thy moste precious heart bloud for me, suffering for my sake, so many & so extreame paines & moste gréeuous torments? Yea, and haste thou not giuen thine owne deare life and soule, to purchase me vnto thy selfe, and to liue with thée in thy fathers kingdome. And nowe to relieue or recouer me out of daunger, shouldest thou shew thy selfe so vnkinde vnto me, that I can not be partaker of thy superfluous store, thine ouerplus and thine offalles? Thy father did so plentifully enriche thée, with so many his worthy graces, to the end, thou (O Lord)

Fayth in Christes bloud.

Lord) shuldest behold in this world
the sicknesse and great necessities of
thy troubled flocke, and largely a-
gaine to distribute vnto the in their
pouertie, and to ease them also of
their painefulnesse and infirmitie.
And bicause (O my Lord and sani-
oure) I yéelde and humbly confesse
me, to be one of those poore, miserable, & scabbed shæpe: and acknowledge thée also, the only bountifull,
good and frée phisition: I come therfore boldly, and say thus vnto thée:
O Christ Iesu, as thy mercifull father hath fréely giuen thée vnto me,
with the fulnesse of thine incomparable and heauenly treasures, for
my ready health, wealth & strength
both of body and soule: so I now flée
vnto thée, moste ioyfully embzasing
thée, and in suche wise truste in thy
mercy, that thou shalt to too muche
wrong me, if thou flée from me or

Scabde shepe.

Chryst the
phisitian.

forsake me. Yea Lorde, I say vnto thee, in consideration hereof, thou oughtest not, neither canst thou abandon or cast me out from thee, but retaine & embrace me, for my most ioyful & sauing health. O lord Iesu, suffer me yet a litle to questiō with thee: Was not thou the very same man, the same Lorde, sauiour & god, which by fauour, hauing enriched thine holy Apostles, gauest them also in charge, that they shuld communicate, deale, and deuide to others such spirituall ryches & heauenly treasures, as thou before haddest giuen vnto them. Should I iudge of thee that giuest coniaunt pennce to others in doing any things, that thou thy selfe wilte not perfourme the same: O Lord, as thou art a god of mercy & truth, and delightest of all men to be truly so noted, were it possible for thee

to

Christ humbly chalenged.

to alter one iot of thy puritie, most
perfect & beautiful clerenesse of thy
godly & diuine nature, wherby one
shæpe of thy flock shoulo quaylæ oz
find any light occasiõ of offence. O
Jesu, as y art righteous, so art not
thou a stübling block vnto the righ
teous. And truly my soule trusteth
in thæ: it moũteth vp into the hea=
uẽs befoze thæ, & my faith is liuely
towards thæ. O perfozme therfoze
faythfully towards me (as thou art
faithful) y which thou didst so iustly
cõmaund vnto thine Apostles and
to vs. Thou certainly doest know
that thine heuẽly father (at the be=
ginning) filled thæ withal vertues,
stuffed thæ with al tresures, poured
his graces vpon thæ with al plen=
tifulnesse : to the ende that in thys
wozld thou shouldest not bend noz
set thy mind, pzoperly to possesse &
gather treasure foz thine own self:

Strong fayth in Chryste.

P.iij.   but

but that thou shouldest altogither, turne and apply thine endeuoure, to see me and the rest of thy poore brethren comforted, safely nourished, kept, strengthened and defended in all assayes. And so thou haste done hitherto, as S. Paule beareth vs in hande: for all that thou hast pretended, wrought and suffered from the beginning, was for me, for thine, and my brethrens sake. Thine holy incarnation therefore, thy natiuitie and circumcision, thy baptisme, thy fasting and praying, thy temptations, thy watchings, thy preachings, thy painful trauellings and dangers, thy shamelesse accusatiõs, spittings and raylings, thy bloudie sweat, thy woful and bitter teares, thy cruel and traiterous apprehension, thy crosse and moste painefull passion, thy bloud shed, thy life, thy death, thy buriall, thy resurrection, yea

Rom, 15.

Chrysts incarnation, natiuitie, & so forth, are al chalenged of the faithfull soule as his owne.

yea & thy moste glozious ascention,
into euerlasting life, and al the rest
which thou haste done, felt, and suffered, was all for me, they are all
mine, and I now chalenge them all
at thine hand, as mine owne. Al thy
diuine treasures are mine: yea, and
euen thou thy selfe art wholely also mine. Thy father hath giuen thée   Rom. 8.
vnto me, and thou also was contented that I should possesse thée, and
therfoze thou canst not nowe denie
thy selfe to be mine . Thou camest   Math. 10.
into this woz lde to take paynes foz
me, and to serue me: and doste thou
not knowe, that what so euer the
seruaunt getteth by his trauaile, he   Chryst a ser-
gaineth it, not foz him selfe, but foz   uaunt.
the vse of hym whome he serueth.
Thou didst like a puissant Pzince,   Chryst a con-
triumphantly fighte foz me, by wa-   querour.
ging and winning battail: and therfoze the treasures and spoyles, the
V.b.   tri-

triumphs and victozies, which thou
then didst get, are altogither mine.
It is not now of late O Iesu, (thou
moste victozious and noble Pzince)
since thou, as with whom were only lefte these greate and pzecious
treasures : and haste thou nowe bestowed them all? I will not say
thine, but my treasures: wherewith
thou hast purchased foz me a moste
pleasant place of rest, euen the ioyfull and heauenly Paradise? yea,
thou haste also taken possession of it
foz me: and shouldest thou now goe
aboute to dispossesse me of myne
owne, and to depziue me of mine
inheritaunce and right? No Lozde
no, there is in me no possibilitie at
all to beléue that: foz I haue (in
suche wise) bothe hearde, felte, and
knowne, diuersly and innumerable
wayes, of thy gratious good nature,
and of thy perfecte charitie and
truthe,

Paradise pur-chased by Christe,

Experience of Christes good nature, and his mercie.

truthe, that I muste nædes confesse
thy great goodnesse and liberalitie
towardes me, and so to trust truely
in thée. Thou hast diligently sought
for me, thou haste offered thy selfe
vnto me, thou hast so many wayes
called vnto me, and so diuers and
sundry wayes allured me to come
to thy moste royal and magnificent
marriage, promising to accepte me,
for thy deare beloued gheast : therefore, I am moste certainely persuaded and fully assured, not to be
deceiued of thée. And thou hast sayd:
he that commeth to thée, thou wilte
not cast him qute,

    And nowe, that I moste gladly
and willingly yéelde vnto thée, and
of good heart come towardes thée,
wilt thou turne thy face away from
me, and not cheare me with thy
comfortable & swéete countenance?
As I am constrained, and by thy
          swéete

Math.xj.xxij.

Iohn.6

Diuine Meditations.

ſwéete allurementes perſuaded, or
rather enforced (beholdyng myne
owne imperfection) to come vnto
thée, that arte altogither perfecte:
euen ſo arte thou (by thy large pro-
miſſes) bounde to accept me. Thou
ſiddeſt ſay : If I ſhall once be exalted, I will then draw all things vnto me. Thine exaltation vppon the
croſſe (O Lord) hath béene (as I beléeue) long ſince perfourmed, as alſo
thy riſing againe from deathe, and
thine aſcention into heauen. Theſe
things therefore, thus truly of thée
perfourmed and finiſhed, I requyre
thée (O Ieſu) to draw me vnto thée,
as thou by thy promiſſe arte moſte
iuſtly bounde. I knowe thou arte
not angrie, or (at the leaſte) not at
defiance with me : for ſéeing thou
haſte commaunded me, that I be
not at hatred with mine enemie : I
can not doubt, but that thou thy ſelf
alſo,

Ioh̄.12.

also, keepest truely this thy sweete commaundement: and so much the rather to be perfourmed of thee, as thou arte moze able than I, to expzesse the vse of charitie. Thou canst not say, that thou art not bounde to loue me, alleaging that I am thine ennemie, oz that I haue done thee manifolde iniuries (which I muste needes moste truely confesse:) foz if by thy pzecept of charitie, thou hast straightly bounde me to loue myne enemies, to doe them good, to helpe them in their neede, and to pzay vnto God foz them: I know right wel that in thus doing, thou arte muche moze bounde than I. Wherefoze, if thou wilt not loue me as thy frend, loue me yet (at the leaste) as thyne enemie: doe me good, help me in my necessities, and pzay to thine heauenly father foz me, as thou art in dede moste bound to doe. I doe assuredly know,

Math. 5.

know, that thy vertue, thy goodnes, and thine heauenly charitie is not so small, nor so slenderly planted in thee, that it will suffer it selfe to be ouercome of mine extreme vnkindnes or naughtinesse: no, how greatly so euer it aboundeth. Thy commaundement chargeth me, that I (in any wise) suffer not my selfe to be vanquished, by the malice of my enemies: and wilte thou suffer thy selfe to be ouercome, by my disfrétship & leudnesse. This verily hathe no likenesse of truth in it. Thou hast taught and commaunded me, that I with doing good to mine enemies, do ouercome and vanquish their malice: and I then require thee (O my mercifull Lord and onely sauieure) that thou also thy selfe, obserue this diuine precept and commaundemét of God thy father, as thy godly nature bindeth thee. Paie thy debte I pray

Roma. 1.

pray thee: that is, vanquish my vain stoutnesse, my wickednesse & great malice, with the vertue of gentlenesse, and with thy most bounteous and plentifull goodnesse. And if I haue an harte before thee, hardened as the Adamant rock or Diamond: breake it then or mollifie it (I beseeche thee) with the piercing moysture of thy moste pretious bloude: O keepe mine heart well therein, souple it, make it softe, and temper it with the moisture of thy grace. O lette thy Spirite then for euer possesse me, henceforthe assiste me, and be my moste gratious and good guide, that I may vntill the ende, obey thy moste holy wil. O worke mine harte a newe, after thine accustomed manner, and according to thy good promisses of olde.

And if thou answeare, that thou hast many times mercifully forgiue me:

Christes payment, and howe.

Ezech 16.

Ezech. 16.

Math 18.

Sinne of Gods electe.

me : and that thou therefore wilte looke no more vppon me, or harken to my sute. I answere: If thou gaueſt Peter in commaundemente, that he ſhould pardon his enemies, not ſeuen times onely, but ſeuentie times ſeuen times:that is alwayes, and as often as they ſhall offende him: It foloweth then,that thou alſo arte ſo muche the more bounde héerein than I, for as much as thou doſte excéede me and all men, in all charitie : and ſpecially,bicauſe that I haue ſinned, not of any deadely malice, but thorowe ignorance and frailtie, and for that bothe I and others,ſawe not rightly the maieſtie of him,whome we ſo offended,ney-ther coulde we make a right biewe of the goodes which we did loſe, nor of the euils, in which we daily did incurre.But thou peraduſiture wilt yet ſay:I haue giuen thée ſuch plen-
tie

tie of lighte and true doctrine, by
sending my faithfull preachers and
ministers these many yeres vnto
thee, that thou art now without excuse, and thy faulte inexcusable.
Agaynst this do I yet replie: that
euen to the Iewes (thy peculier
people) thou gauest suche lights to
sée, and such knowledge to perceiue
what thou was, that they were yet
inexcusable, as thou thy selfe dyd-
dest say. And notwithstanding this,
thou béeing in triumphe vppon the
Crosse, diddest make their excuse,
and prayed for them, saying : that
in putting thée to that cruell death,
they knew not what they dyd. In
consideration of which things, séeing thou art myne onely aduocate,
myne onely Sauiour, my God and
dearely beloued of thy father, my
trust is in thée, that thou wilt haue
mercy vppon me, and pray for me.

I.

Iohn.15.

thyte the
onely saulour,
the onely ad-
uocate.

O pray for me therefore I beſœche thœ, make myne excuſe to thyne and myne heauenly father: O ſaue thou me, and then ſhall I bœ ſafe. And if thou wilte yet lay to my charge (O thou iuſte God) that I haue with earneſt ſtoutneſſe and rebellion offended thœ: myne anſwere agayne vnto thœ is (whych ſœſt the ſecrotes of myne hearte) that in ſo doing I haue done it, not wilfully and of malice, but rather of frayltie, or through feruencie of zeale, with all ſingleneſſe of heart, to ſœke onely thy glory. Wherein through wante of knowledge, and the true lighte of thy holy Goſpell, I haue diſobediently and ſtubbornly committed iniquitie: but yet, not in ſuche wyſe as doth the damned reprobate, fixedly, of wylfull malice, or as an hater of thœ: who by all poſſible meanes ſœketh thy diſho-

Sinne of the reprobate.

dishonour, and falleth with al gree-
dynesse from iniquitie to iniquitie.
Therefore I doubte not but suche
zeale or frayltie ioyned with sim-
plenesse, is pardonable before thee,
through the gretnesse of thy mercy:
yea, it is so much the more to the
furtherance of thy glory (o Christ)
rather than the only offences committed of meere simplicitie, when
the largenesse of thy mercyes so
bountifully floweth from thee. Yea,
and I know assuredly, that throgh
thy goodnesse and feruent charitie,
thou art inforced to vanquishe and
vtterly ouerthrow my weakenesse,
wickednesse, malice and blindnesse,
euen to the pardoning of all (from
the firste to the laste) that hathe
beene amisse. For if the iuste bloud
of Abell called to God for venge-
aunce agaynst his brother to hys
condemnation, and preuayled, I
know

The bloud of Abel cried for vengeance.

know that thy bloud muche moze
effectually calleth to saluation:and
calling, obteineth abounbaunce of
Gods mercies foz me. Saue me
therefoze (O my Lozde and sweete
Jesu) accozding to thy pzomyses
and bonde of great charitie:against
the whiche, neither thou oughtest
noz canst resiste. O saue me J be=
seeche thee,and take me to thy mer=
cy, sometime one of thy great eni=
mies,very wicked, very faithlesse,
obstinate, headie and rebellious:
but nowe thy louing bzother, thy
faythfull frende, thyne obediente
louer, and a sounde member of thy
body. O saue me then J say, com=
fozte my soule, guyde mee in thy
wayes, strengthen mee, and let
not thy spirite departe from mee,
that J may hencefozthe ioyfully
please thee, and render alwayes
vnto thy father (thzough thee) all
due

due prayſe, honour, and glory, here
in thys vale of myſerie, and
in the euerlaſting world
which is to come.
Amen.

F I N I S.

¶Imprinted at Lon-
don by Henry Bynneman,
for William Norton.

ANNO. 1572.

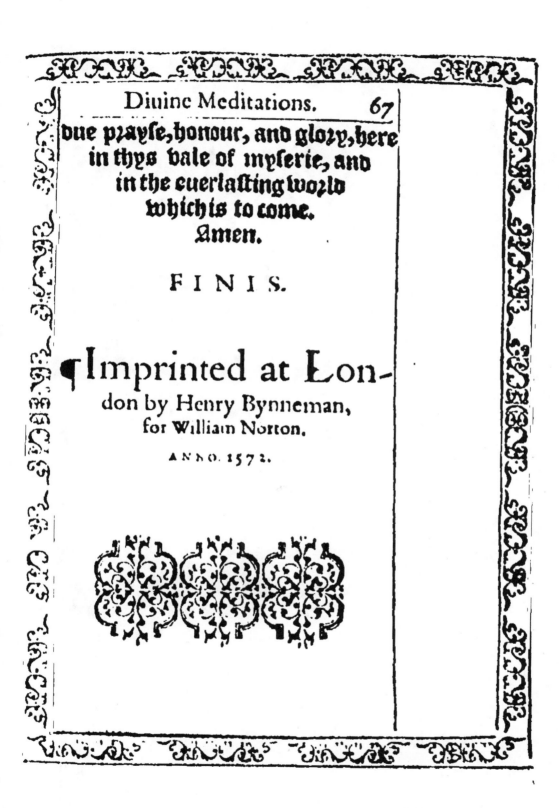

CPSIA information can be obtained
at www.ICGtesting.com
Printed in the USA
BVHW09s1424131018
530026BV00005B/399/P